Science NG
Student Guide

3

K12 Summit
CURRICULUM

About K12 Inc.
K12 Inc. (NYSE: LRN) drives innovation and advances the quality of education by delivering state-of-the-art digital learning platforms and technology to students and school districts around the world. K12 is a company of educators offering its online and blended curriculum to charter schools, public school districts, private schools, and directly to families. More information can be found at K12.com.

978-1-60153-596-2

Printed by Bradford & Bigelow, Newburyport, MA, USA, September 2020

Table of Contents

Student Guide

Introduction to the Musculoskeletal System

Why don't we flop around like jellyfish on land? Because our bones and muscles work together to hold our parts upright. They also allow us to move ourselves and other things around.

Lesson Objectives

- Explain that bones, cartilage, tendons, and ligaments make up the skeletal system.
- Recognize that cells form tissues, tissues form organs, organs form body systems, and systems work together to make up the human body.
- Compare the movement of various joints.
- Identify the functions of joints, ligaments, tendons, and cartilage.
- State three main functions of the skeletal system: support, protection of internal organs, and movement.

PREPARE

Approximate lesson time is 60 minutes.

Keywords and Pronunciation

cartilage (KAHR-tl-ij)**:** Strong, flexible tissue that forms the skeleton of some fish. A shark's skeleton is not hard and bony, but is made of flexible cartilage.

joint: A point where two bones meet, and which generally make movement possible. Knuckles are one kind of finger joint.

ligament: A sheet or band of tough, fibrous tissue connecting bones or cartilage at a joint or supporting an organ. We have ligaments in our leg joints.

musculoskeletal (muhs-kyuh-loh-SKEH-luh-tl)

musculoskeletal system: a system of the body made of the muscles and skeleton

tendon: A band of tough, inelastic fibrous tissue that connects a muscle with a bone. Tendons help our muscles move our bones.

vertebrae (VUR-tuh-bray)**:** The small bones that make up the backbone. The bumps you feel in your back are your vertebrae.

LEARN

Activity 1: Bones and Muscles Work Together *(Online)*

Activity 2: How Do Joints Move? *(Offline)*

There are many joints in the skeletal system. The joints let your body move in different ways. Think about how your body moves and where it bends.

There are four different types of joints that help your body move:

1. Ball-and-socket joint - allows your body to move in all directions. Your shoulder and upper arm are connected at a ball-and-socket joint.

2. Hinge joint - allows your bones to move backward and forward in only one direction. Bend your arm at the elbow. This is a hinge joint.

3. Gliding joint - allows your joints to move in many directions. In gliding joints, the bones slide along each other. If you move your wrist, you will see a gliding joint in action.

4. Pivot joint - allows movement in a circular path like a swivel chair. If you look side-to-side, you will see how a pivot joint helps you move.

Take a piece of paper and fold it in half. Fold it in half again so that the paper is divided into four equal pieces. Label one square "Pivot Joints." Label the others with "Ball-and-Socket Joints," "Gliding Joints," and "Hinge Joints."

Start by bending your leg at the knee. What type of joint is that? [1] Write "knee" in the box labeled "Hinge Joint." Now move the different joints of your body and decide which type of joint each is. Record the body part in the box that matches the type of joint that helps it move.

ASSESS

Lesson Assessment: Introduction to the Musculoskeletal System *(Offline)*

Sit with an adult to review the assessment questions.

Student Guide

Bone Identification

Bones let us stand upright. How else do bones help the body? Explore the bones in the human body to find out what they do.

Lesson Objectives

- Demonstrate mastery of important knowledge and skills taught in previous lessons.
- Classify bones by function: support, protection, or movement.
- Classify bones by shape: long, short, flat, and irregular.
- Identify five of the many bones of the skeletal system.
- State that bone cells and tissue are formed as cartilage is replaced.

PREPARE

Approximate lesson time is 60 minutes.

Materials

For the Student

>Bone Sort
>Skeleton Concentration

Keywords and Pronunciation

radius: Long, slightly curved bone, the shorter and thicker of the two forearm bones, located on the opposite side of the ulna.

cartilage (KAHR-tl-ij)**:** Strong, flexible tissue that forms the skeleton of some fish. A shark's skeleton is not hard and bony, but is made of flexible cartilage.

Cranium: The portion of the skull enclosing the brain.

Femur: A bone of the upper leg, found between the pelvis and knee in humans.

femur (FEE-mur)

fibula (FIH-byuh-luh)

Humerus: The long bone of the arm, extending from the shoulder to the elbow.

Phalanges: The finger bones.

phalanges (fuh-LAN-jeez)

Scapula: Either of two large, flat, triangular bones forming the back part of the shoulder. Also called the shoulder blade.

Tibia: The inner and larger of the two bones of the lower human leg, extending from the knee to the ankle.

tibia (TIH-bee-uh)

Ulna: The bone extending from the elbow to the wrist on the side opposite the thumb in humans.

Vertebra: Any of the bones forming the spinal column.

vertebrae (VUR-tuh-bray)**:** The small bones that make up the backbone. The bumps you feel in your back are your vertebrae.

LEARN

Activity 1: Types of Bones *(Online)*

Activity 2: Bone Sort *(Offline)*

Look at the skeleton of the human body. There are 206 bones that make it up. Each has its own job to do. Bones act as support. They also help the body move. Many bones protect the organs of the body, such as the brain, heart and lungs.

1. Cut out each of the sets of bones.

2. Cut out each label: support, movement, and protection.

3. Look at each bone set. Decide whether it provides support, movement or protection for the body.

4. Place the bone set under the appropriate heading.

5. Check your answers to see if they match the listed ones below.

Now choose three different colored crayons to represent three functions of bones—support, movement, and protection.

Locate support bones on the skeleton. Color them one color. Then find protection bones. Color them another color. Then color bones that help the body with movement.

Answers:

Protection: clavicle, skull, sternum, patella

Movement: phalanges of the hand, phalanges of the foot

Support: ribs, femur, tibia, fibula

Note: some bones may have more than one function, so answers may vary. For instance, ribs protect and support.

Activity 3: Skeleton Concentration *(Offline)*

Read the following game rules.

Cut out the cards with the letters and bone names. Lay all cards face down and shuffle them around.

Let's begin. The goal of the game is to match the letters with their respective bone names, as illustrated in the skeleton sheet. Turn over one card, then turn over another card. Do these cards match? If the cards do not match, lay the second card face down again. Turn over cards until you find the right match. When you do find a match—for example, the letter B and skull— leave the cards face up. Continue playing until all letters and bone names have been matched.

ASSESS

Lesson Assessment: Bone Identification *(Online)*

You will complete an online assessment covering the main objectives of the lesson.

Name _____ Date _____

Bone Identification

Bone Sort

Look at the skeleton of the human body. There are 206 bones that make up the skeleton. Each has their own job to do. Bones can act as support for the body. They can also help the body move. Many bones also protect the organs of the body - like the brain, heart and lungs.

1. Cut out each of the sets of bones.

2. Cut out each label: support, movement, and protection.

3. Look at each bone set. Decide whether it provides support, movement or protection for the body.

4. Place the bone set under the appropriate heading.

5. Check your answers to see if you were right.

Support
Movement
Protection

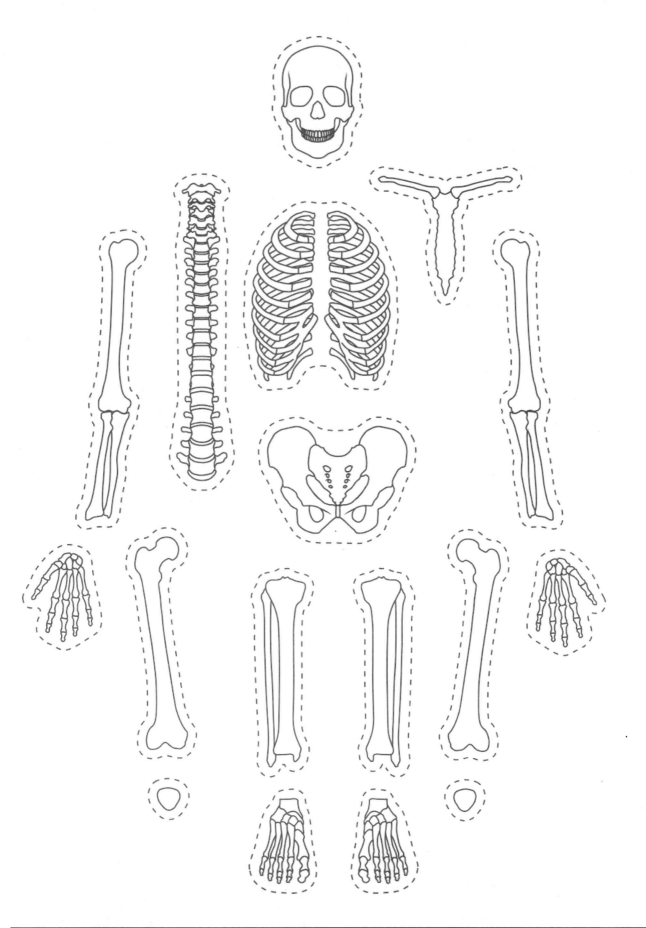

Now choose three different colored crayons to represent the three functions of bones - support, movement and protection.

Locate the support bones on the skeleton. Color them one color. Then find the protection bones. Color them another color. Then color the bones that help the body with movement.

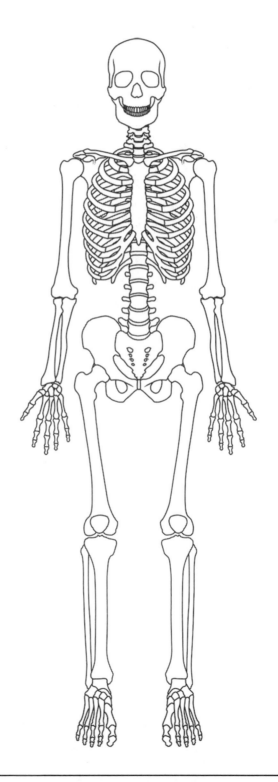

Name _____   Date _____

Bone Identification

Skeleton Concentration

1. Cut out the cards with the letters and bone names.

2. Lay all cards face down and shuffle them around.

3. Let's begin. The goal of the game is to match the letters with their respective bone names, as illustrated in the skeleton sheet. Turn over one card, then turn over another card. Do these cards match? If the cards do not match, lay the second card face down again. Turn over as many cards until you find the right match. When you do find a match, for example, the letter B and skull, leave the cards face up.

A	clavicle
B	skull
C	sternum
D	ribs
E	phalanges of the hand
F	patella
G	phalanges of the feet

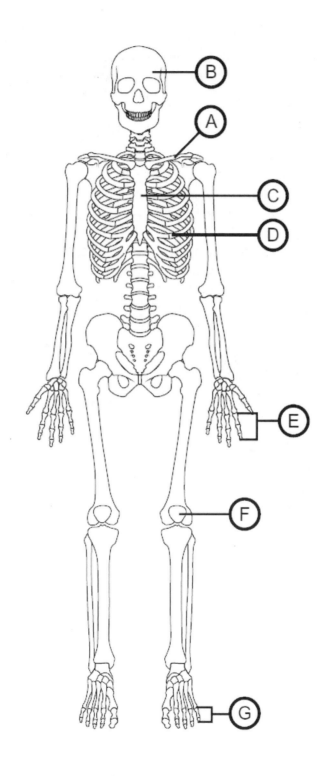

Student Guide
Bone Structure

Bones come in many shapes and sizes. Bones help protect, support, and move the body. But what are bones made of? Why are they hard? Why are they light? Learn about the structure and the functions of different types of bones. Then make a model and discover the important parts of bones.

Lesson Objectives

- Explain how the structure of bones makes bones both strong and light.
- Identify two types of bone tissue: compact and spongy.
- Recognize that bones are made up of various types of cells, blood vessels, nerves, and minerals like calcium.
- Explain that red marrow forms blood cells and is located in the cavities of spongy bone.
- Explain that yellow bone marrow stores fats and is located in the hollow section of long bones of adults, surrounded by compact bone.

PREPARE

Approximate lesson time is 60 minutes.

Advance Preparation

- Purchase uncooked bread dough, puffed rice cereal, and blue yarn. Your student will use thinly rolled dough to make a model of a bone.
- Cook the chicken leg before beginning the activity with your student.

Keywords and Pronunciation

cartilage (KAHR-tl-ij)**:** Strong, flexible tissue that forms the skeleton of some fish. A shark's skeleton is not hard and bony, but is made of flexible cartilage.

compact bone: The hard, outside part of the bone that gives the bone its strength.

femur (FEE-mur)

growth plate: A plate of cartilage located near each end of long bones of growing children and teens. Growth plates gradually disappear as the cartilage is replaced by bone and growth stops.

irregular bone: A bone that is not classified as long, short, or flat, often with a complex shape. The vertebrae and the bones of the inner ear are irregular bones.

marrow: The substance filling marrow cavities in the bone. Red marrow makes blood cells (including red and white blood cells). Yellow marrow stores fat.

mineral: A naturally occurring element—such as calcium, iron, potassium, sodium, or zinc—or compound. Many minerals are necessary for the nutrition and growth of humans, other animals, and plants.

spongy bone: Light bone tissue that contains open spaces. Spongy bone is also strong because its bony connections give it support.

LEARN

Activity 1: The Structure of Bones *(Online)*

Activity 2: Make a Bone Model *(Offline)*

Instructions

Overview

In this activity, you will make a model of two parts of a long bone, the long tube-like shaft, and the knobby end. You will make each part, then put them together to represent the two parts of a long bone connected together.

The toilet-paper tube will represent the hollow center of the bone. Puffed rice will represent bone cells, the colored clay will represent bone marrow, the dough will represent the mineralized bone, and the blue strands will represent nerves and blood vessels.

Activity Steps

A. Make the tubular shaft

1. More or less fill the center of the tube with yellow clay. This will be the yellow bone marrow.

2. Wrap a thin layer of dough around the tube. Lay a couple of strands of blue yarn across the dough. Separate the strands as you do this. These will be woven in with the dough and puffed rice to represent the blood vessels that bring or transport nutrients to the bone.

3. Roll the dough in scattered puffed rice so that the rice covers the dough and the blue yarn. The rice represents living cells scattered throughout the bone.

4. Apply another layer of dough, then more puffed rice. Be sure to "weave" the veins and arteries through the layers. Alternate the layers until the model is about 4 cm thick from the center (about 8 cm total diameter, across the widest part, including the yellow marrow cavity). This represents the compact bone layer.

5. Apply a smooth layer of dough to the outside of the bone.

B. Make the knobby head

1. Make little balls of red clay, about 1/2 centimeter across (they don't need to be exactly round). They will represent red marrow.

2. Place some of these balls close together on a circular piece of dough about 5 centimeters in diameter. Cover them with another layer of dough. Push the dough between the balls, and embed some puffed rice in the dough (add more dough, if necessary), then add more balls. Continue until this structure is about 2 centimeters thick, ending with a layer of dough.

3. This last layer should cover the whole piece except one edge where you will leave the red marrow exposed to have a "cutaway" view of the inside.

C. Connect the shaft to the knobby head

1. Take this piece and place it on one end of the tube, with the cutaway edge over the yellow marrow cavity. This represents spongy bone at the end of a long bone, with red marrow in the cavities.

2. Place a piece of masking tape at the top of the toothpick. Write the names of the following parts of the bone on a toothpick flag: yellow bone marrow, compact bone layer, blood vessels, cells, spongy bone layer, and red bone marrow. Place each flag on the model to identify the part shown on the flag.

Good job! You've just created your own masterpiece bone model.

Note: Refrigerate the bone model to save it for the Unit Assessment in lesson 10 of this unit.

Safety

This lesson involves working with food. Before beginning, check with your doctor, if necessary, to find out whether your student will have any allergic reactions.

Be careful when using sharp tools.

ASSESS

Lesson Assessment: Bone Structure (*Online*)

You will complete an online assessment covering the main objectives of the lesson.

LEARN

Activity 3: Why Are Bones Hard? (*Offline*)

Instructions

Overview

In this activity you will have the chance to see what happens when the minerals in bones are removed over time. You will use a cooked chicken leg to watch the neat changes.

Steps

3. *Adult only*: Remove as much of the meat from the bone as possible.

4. Wash the bone in soapy water and rinse it thoroughly.

5. Gently try to bend the bone, but be careful not to break it (it should not bend much at this stage, if at all.)

6. Place the bone in the jar with the vinegar. Put the lid on.

7. After 24 hours, remove the bone with tongs, rinse it off, and carefully try to bend it again. Is the bone easier to bend?

8. Repeat steps 4-5 once a day for one week.

Conclusion

The calcium in bones makes them hard and not easily bent. Over time, the vinegar takes the calcium out of the bone and the bone becomes bendable. Without calcium, our bones would not be able to support us or move as a unit.

Student Guide
Joints in the Human Body

There are many types of joints that allow the human body to move. Review the four main types of joints and examples of each. Then, do an experiment with your thumb to discover the importance of this joint.

Lesson Objectives

- Describe the following types of joints: hinge, ball-and-socket, gliding, and pivot.
- Locate an example of each type of joint (hinge, ball-and-socket, gliding, and pivot) in the body.
- Evaluate the function of joints by restricting a joint, such as the thumb.

PREPARE

Approximate lesson time is 60 minutes.

Materials

For the Student

What Kind of Joint Is It?
I Can't Live Without My Thumb!

Keywords and Pronunciation

ball-and-socket joint: A place where bones meet that lets the joint move in all directions. Your shoulder is a ball-and-socket joint.

cartilage (KAHR-tl-ij)**:** Strong, flexible tissue that forms the skeleton of some fish. A shark's skeleton is not hard and bony, but is made of flexible cartilage.

femur (FEE-mur)

gliding joint: A place where bones meet and slide or glide along each other. Gliding joints don't allow as much movement as ball-and-socket or hinge joints, but they do allow small movements in many directions.

hinge joint: A place where bones meet that allows them to move back and forth like the hinge of a door, but not to twist around.

humerus (HYOO-mur-uhs)

ligaments: Tough bands of tissue that connect bones to one another.

marrow: Soft tissue found inside most bones. Red marrow produces blood cells, and yellow marrow stores fat.

phalanges (fuh-LAN-jeez)

pivot joint: A place where bones meet that allows for turning in a circular motion.

scapula (SKA-pyuh-luh)

tendons: Strong bands of tissue that attach muscles to bones.

tibia (TIH-bee-uh)

vertebra (VUR-tuh-bruh)

LEARN

Activity 1: Understanding Our Joints *(Online)*

Explore the different types of joints in the human body. Gain an understanding of how various types of joints move.

Activity 2: What Kind of Joint Is It? *(Offline)*

Part I

There are four major types of joints in the human body: ball-and-socket, gliding, pivot, and hinge. Look back through the Explore to find each type. Then, below the joint name, write a description of how the joint moves.

Pivot

Ball-and-socket

Hinge

Gliding

Part II

Now let's make a model of one type of joint, the ball-and-socket joint.

1. Make a round clay ball the size of your fist.

2. Mold the clay so that it looks like a bowl. This is the *socket* part of the joint.

3. Use another piece of clay to create a round ball that will fit inside the clay bowl. The ball should not touch the sides or the bottom of the bowl.

4. Attach a cylinder-shaped piece of clay to the *ball*. This represents the *shaft* of the bone with a ball-shaped end. The end of the cylinder should reach above the top of the bowl. This is the ball part of the joint.

Let's see how the model of the ball-and-socket joint moves. Can you rotate the ball in a circle? Can you move it from one side straight across to the other? Is there anything that keeps it from moving in a certain direction?

Conclusion

Your shoulder and arm meet at a ball-and-socket joint. The top end of your upper arm bone (humerus) is shaped like a round ball at the end. This ball-shaped end fits into a cup-shaped socket on your shoulder blade (scapula). The ball rolls around inside the socket. The socket, along with ligaments, keeps the joint together.

Activity 3: I Can't Live Without My Thumb! *(Offline)*

Activity Steps

1. Hold your fingers straight out and close to each other.

2. Have someone tape your thumb to the side of your hand by wrapping tape around your whole hand so that you cannot move your thumb. Do the same to the other hand.

Now let's see what important job the thumb does! Try to pick up your pencil and write your name. Was it easy? Hard? How about trying to eat your dinner with a spoon or fork? Can you do that easily? Now experiment with other jobs that you use your hands for.

Describe the importance of your thumb joint in doing everyday activities.

ASSESS

Lesson Assessment: Joint in the Human Body *(Online)*

You will complete an online assessment covering the main objectives of the lesson.

Name _____   Date _____

Joints in the Human Body
What Kind of Joint Is It?

Part 1

There are four major types of joints in the human body: ball-and-socket, gliding, pivot, and hinge. Look back through the Explore to find each type. Then, below the joint name, write a description of how the joint moves. Include examples of each joint too.

1. Pivot

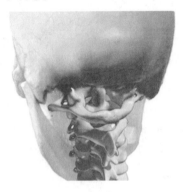

_____

_____

2. Ball-and-socket

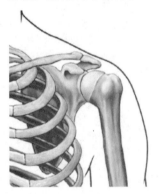

_____

_____

3. Hinge

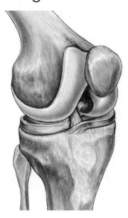

_____

_____

4. Gliding

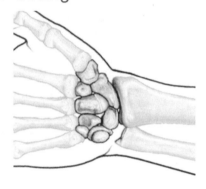

_____

_____

Part 2

Now let's make a model of one type of joint, the ball-and-socket joint.

1. Make a round clay ball the size of your fist.

2. Mold the clay so that it looks like a bowl. This is the socket part of the joint.

3. Use another piece of clay to create a round ball that will fit inside the clay bowl. The ball should not touch the sides or the bottom of the bowl.

4. Attach a cylinder-shaped piece of clay to the ball. This represents the shaft of the bone with a ball-shaped end. The end of the cylinder should reach above the top of the bowl. This is the ball part of the joint.

5. Let's see how the model of the ball-and-socket joint moves. Can you rotate the ball in a circle? Can you move it from one side straight across to the other? Is there anything that keeps it from moving in a certain direction?

Name _____   Date _____

Joints in the Human Body
I Can't Live Without My Thumb!

Activity Steps

1. Hold your fingers straight out and close to each other.

2. Have someone tape your thumb to the side of your hand by wrapping tape around your whole hand so your thumb cannot move. Do the same to the other hand.

3. Now let's see what important job the thumb plays! Try to pick up your pencil and write your name. Was it easy? Hard? How about trying to eat your dinner with a spoon or fork? Can you do that easily? Now experiment with other jobs that you use your hands for.

4. Describe the importance of your thumb joint in doing everyday activities.

_____

_____

_____

_____

_____

_____

_____

_____

Student Guide

Optional: Broken Bones

Many people break bones in their body while doing everyday activities like walking, riding a bicycle, running, and climbing trees. What does a broken bone look like under the skin? How does the bone get repaired? Learn more about what doctors see in X-rays that helps them treat broken bones.

Lesson Objectives

- Describe how a broken bone heals.
- Identify tools used to detect and treat a broken bone, such as X-rays, casts, and splints.
- Identify two types of bone fractures, such as open and closed.

PREPARE

Approximate lesson time is 60 minutes.

Materials

For the Student

> X-Ray Diagnosis
> First Aid for Broken Bones

Keywords and Pronunciation

bowing (BOH-ing)

cast: A hard sleeve that is placed around a body part to help heal a broken bone. The cast keeps the broken bone from moving around once it has been set.

fracture (FRAK-chuhr): A broken bone. The X-ray showed the fracture in my arm after I fell from the tree.

setting a bone: Placing broken pieces of bone back together in their normal positions so they can heal in a proper shape and position.

splint: A thin strip of metal, plastic, or wood that is taped onto the body part. A splint keeps the broken bone in place to help it heal.

LEARN

Activity 1: Optional: Lesson Instructions (*Online*)

Activity 2: Optional: Healing Bones (*Online*)

Activity 3: Optional: X-Ray Diagnosis (*Online*)

Activity 4: Optional: First Aid for Broken Bones *(Offline)*

If you're not careful, an accident around the house, such as falling off a bike, tripping while running, or falling during a game of basketball could cause a fracture. That's why safety experts and your parents remind you to wear a helmet when you are riding your bike, and to make sure you tie your shoelaces. These things help keep you safe. But sometimes a fracture can occur. What should you do if you break a bone? One type of first aid for a fracture is to place it in a splint until you can have a doctor treat it. Pretend you have fractured your arm. Let's see how a splint works on an arm!

Activity Steps

1. Find an object around the house that will work as a splint. Anything that is straight, including cardboard, a rolled-up newspaper, wooden boards, a broom handle, or a cane, will work. The splint should be longer than your arm bone and joint you want to support.

2. If you chose a hard object, pad the splint with soft material such as a piece of clothing or blanket.

3. Place the splint under your arm, between your wrist and elbow. Use several scarves or pieces of fabric to wrap the padded splint to your arm. It should fit snugly but should not cut off blood circulation.

4. Once you have your arm in the splint, place an ice bag over the area of the break. Place the ice bag over a towel, not directly on the skin.

Now you can pretend to visit the doctor's office for a diagnosis. Is your arm broken? An X-ray will help the doctor tell if you will need a cast. A cast is made of many different materials. Its job is to keep the broken bone in place so it can heal correctly.

Extension

Use the same steps in the activity to make a splint for a broken leg or finger.

Name _____   Date _____

Broken Bones

X-Ray Diagnosis

X-rays are taken to show where a bone may be broken. There are many different types of bone fractures. The name of each type of fracture describes the way the bones look in an X-ray. All fractures are either open or closed. An open fracture is one in which the broken bone pokes through the skin. In a closed fracture the bone breaks but doesn't come through the skin.

Go back into the Explore and find the pictures of the types of fractures listed below. Then draw your own X-ray that shows that type of fracture.

1. open fracture

2. closed fracture

Name _____   Date _____

Broken Bones

First Aid for Broken Bones

An accident around the house, such as falling off a bike, tripping while running or falling while playing a game of basketball could cause a fracture if you're not careful. That's why safety experts, and your parents, remind you to wear a helmet when riding your bike and to tie your shoelaces. These things help keep you safe. But sometimes a fracture can occur. What should you do? One type of first aid for a fracture is to create a splint for it. Pretend your arm has been fractured. Let's see how a splint works on an arm.

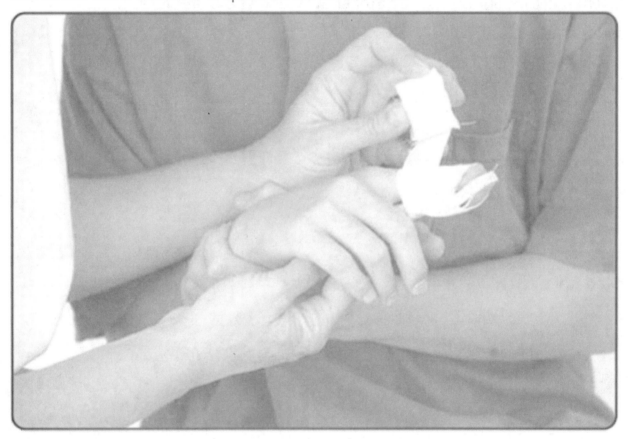

Activity Steps

Find an object around the house that will work as a splint. Anything that is straight, including a rolled-up newspaper, wooden boards, a broom handle or a cane, will work. The splint should be longer than the arm bone and joint you want to support.

1. If you chose a hard object, try to pad the splint with soft material such as a piece of clothing or blanket.

2. Place the splint under the arm, between the wrist and the elbow. Use several scarves or pieces of fabric to wrap the padded splint to the arm. It should fit snugly but should not cut off blood circulation.

3. After the arm has been placed in the splint, place an icebag over the area of the break. Place it over a towel, not directly on the skin.

Now you can (pretend to) visit the doctor's office for a diagnosis. Is it broken? An X-ray will help the doctor find out to see if the arm will need a cast. A cast is made of many different materials. Its job is to keep the broken bone in place so that it can heal correctly.

Student Guide
Types of Muscles

Can we control every movement of our body, including digesting food and pumping blood? Explore the role of voluntary and involuntary muscles and the types of tissue that make up different kinds of muscles.

Lesson Objectives

- Recognize that *voluntary muscles* are muscles you can move when you want to, while *involuntary muscles* are muscles that move automatically.
- Explain the function of the skeletal, smooth, and cardiac muscles.
- Identify the three types of muscles (skeletal, smooth, and cardiac).

PREPARE

Approximate lesson time is 60 minutes.

Materials

For the Student

Exercise Your Heart

Keywords and Pronunciation

cartilage (KAHR-tl-ij): Strong, flexible tissue that forms the skeleton of some fish. A shark's skeleton is not hard and bony, but is made of flexible cartilage.

esophagus (ih-SAH-fuh-guhs)

involuntary muscles: Muscles we are unable to control directly, such as the heart.

voluntary muscles: Muscles we are able to control directly, such as the leg muscles.

LEARN

Activity 1: Muscles of the Body *(Online)*

Activity 2: Voluntary vs. Involuntary Muscles *(Online)*

Activity 3: Exercise Your Heart *(Online)*

Review

Many involuntary muscles have effects on the body that we can actually see. The heart is one such involuntary muscle.

Activity Steps

- Look in the mirror at your face. Notice its color. Then feel your palms, neck, and face. Are you sweating?
- Find your resting pulse rate by timing your heartbeats. Place your index and middle finger on your neck until you feel your pulse. Then count the number of pulses you feel in 10 seconds. Multiply that number by 6 and that is your number of heartbeats per minute. Write your resting pulse rate here.

- Now let's see what exercise does to the heart and body. Run for 5 minutes, in place or outside.
- Look at your face again in the mirror. What color is it now? Are your palms, neck, or face sweating? Take your pulse again and find out what your exercising pulse rate is.

Conclusion

What caused these effects? As your muscles work harder, they need more oxygen, which the heart supplies by moving your blood. Your heart has to beat faster to keep up with your muscles' needs. Your body sweats to release extra heat from exercising. In addition, your face may have become slightly red because the small blood vessels in the skin expand to carry more blood, which also helps to release the heat caused by the exercise.

All these things happened because of one muscle we can't control directly—the heart!

ASSESS

Lesson Assessment: Types of Muscles (*Online*)

You will complete an online assessment covering the main objectives of the lesson.

Name _____ Date _____

Types of Muscles
Exercise Your Heart

Review

Many involuntary muscles have effects on the body that we can actually see. The heart is one of those involuntary muscles.

Activity Steps

1. Look in the mirror at your face. Notice its color. Then feel your palms, neck and face. Are you sweating?

   _____

   _____

2. Find out what your resting pulse rate is. You can time your pulse to measure your heart rate. Place your index and middle fingers on your neck until you feel your pulse. Then count the number of pulses you feel for 10 seconds. Multiply that number by 6 and that is your heartbeats per minute. Write your resting rate pulse here.

   _____

3. Now let's see what exercise does to the heart and your body. Run in place, or outside, for 5 minutes.

4. Look at your face again in the mirror. What color is it now? Are your neck, palms or face sweating? Take your pulse again and find out what your exercising heart rate is.

   _____

   _____

Student Guide

Muscle Action

How do muscles move the human body? Explore how muscles work together with other muscles and also how they work with body parts, especially bones.

Lesson Objectives

- State that most skeletal muscles work in pairs.
- Explain that *flexor muscles* contract to bend joints as *extensor muscles* relax, and *extensor* muscles contract to straighten joints as *flexors* relax.
- State that when a muscle contracts it gets shorter.
- State that your muscles can move your body only by contracting.

PREPARE

Approximate lesson time is 60 minutes.

Materials

For the Student

Extensors and Flexors

Keywords and Pronunciation

cardiac muscle: A type of muscle found only in the heart. Cardiac muscle is involuntary muscle.

contract: To shorten. In the case of a muscle, contracting applies a pulling force to the ends of the muscle. You contract your jaw muscles to bite your sandwich.

extensor: a muscle that, when it contracts, extends or straightens a body part

flexor: a muscle that, when it contracts, bends a body part

involuntary muscle: A muscle that contracts and relaxes automatically, without your telling it to. The muscles that move food through your intestines are involuntary muscles.

skeletal muscle: A type of muscle that attaches to one or more bones, and pulls on a bone or other body part. Skeletal muscle is voluntary muscle.

smooth muscle: A type of muscle found in the walls of the stomach, intestines, and blood vessels (as well as some other places). Smooth muscle is involuntary muscle.

voluntary muscle: A muscle that you can contract or relax on command. You use your voluntary muscles when you play sports.

LEARN

Activity 1: Muscle Action *(Online)*

Activity 2: Extensors and Flexors *(Online)*

ASSESS

Lesson Assessment: Muscle Action *(Offline)*

Sit with an adult to review the assessment questions.

Name _____   Date _____

Muscle Action
Extensors and Flexors

Activity Steps

1. Cut out the foot and leg pattern on the next page.

2. On the leg pattern, use a hole punch to make two holes where the solid dots are.

3. Use the tip of a pencil to make a small hole through each pattern on the places marked with an X.

4. Place the foot pattern on top of the leg pattern, lining up the two holes made with the pencil. Place a brass fastener in the hole to attach the two pieces.

5. Measure two pieces of string, each 30 cm long.

6. Put a piece of string through each punched hole. Tape one end of the string to each square mark on the pattern. The ends of the string closest to the top of the leg should not be taped.

Now let's see how the model works. Carefully pull up on the string that is closest to the toe of the foot. What happens?

_____

_____

Now pull on the string closest to the heel of the foot. What happens then?

_____

_____

Do you see that the muscles have to work as a pair to move your foot both ways?

Conclusion

It's important to remember that the muscles in our bodies are actually getting longer when they relax and shorter when they contract. The entire string in our model doesn't change its length. But you can see that the amount of string showing on each part of the pattern changes as the foot is flexed and then extended, depending on which "muscle" is contracting (less string) or relaxing (more string).

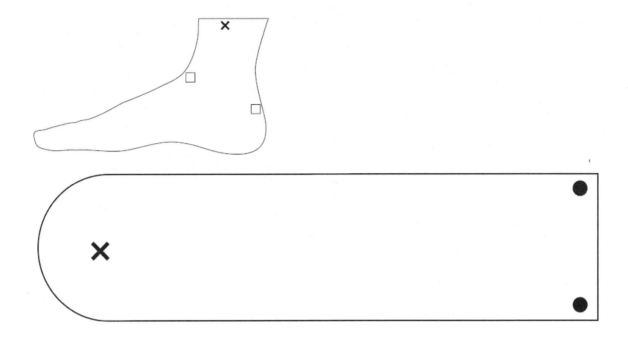

Student Guide
Layers of the Skin

Look down at your hands. What do you see? Even though you can't see anything happening, your skin is busy at work! Your skin covers and protects everything inside your body. Explore the structure and function of your skin.

Lesson Objectives

- Explain the main functions of the skin (protecting against infection, helping keep the body's internal temperature constant, and sensing the environment).
- Identify the skin as the body's largest organ.
- Identify the two main layers of the skin as the epidermis and dermis and explain their main characteristics.
- Recognize that hair and nails are part of the skin system.

PREPARE

Approximate lesson time is 60 minutes.

Materials

For the Student

Investigate Your Skin

Keywords and Pronunciation

dermis: The second layer of skin that contains nerves, blood vessels, oil glands, and sweat glands. The splinter in my finger went into the dermis.

dilate: To widen at an opening. The pupil of the human eye dilates in the darkness to let more light in.

epidermis (eh-puh-DUR-muhs)**:** The outermost skin layer. The epidermis is the layer of skin that you can see.

keratin (KEHR-uh-tn)**:** A tough protein found in nails, hair, and the outer layer of skin. She bought a special type of body lotion that contained aloe and keratin.

sebum (SEE-bum)**:** The oil produced by glands in the skin. Sebum helps make skin waterproof.

LEARN

Activity 1: Skin and Its Layers (Online)

Activity 2: Investigate Your Skin (Offline)

ASSESS

Lesson Assessment: Layers of the Skin (Online)

You will complete an online assessment covering the main objectives of the lesson.

Name _____   Date _____

Layers of the Skin

Investigate Your Skin

Your skin has many jobs to do for the body—protecting it against infection, helping to keep its internal temperature constant, and sensing the environment. But what does it look like up close? Is the skin the same everywhere on our body? Let's find out!

Activity 1: Tape Detective

1. Cut a piece of clear tape about 6 cm long.

2. Place it on the underside of your arm. Rub back and forth on the tape to be sure it has attached to the skin on your arm.

3. Carefully pull the tape off. Look carefully at it. What do you see? Does the tape look the same as the rest on the roll? What do you think is on the tape?

_____

_____

_____

Activity 2: How Did That Get In There?

1. Find a clear plastic bag slightly larger than the size of your hand.

2. Place the bag over one hand.

3. Wrap tape around the opening of the bag and your wrist so that the bag is completely sealed.

4. Watch carefully for about 5 minutes. Do you see anything changing inside the bag? What do you think it is? How did it get there?

_____

_____

_____

_____

Activity 3: Make Your Own Skin Prints

1. Rub a pencil back and forth on the blank white paper. The pencil mark should be about the size of your palm.

2. Rub the inside of your wrist on the pencil markings until it's black.

3. Place a piece of clear tape over your wrist. Then gently lift the tape. Now you will have a print of your skin.

4. Tape your skin print onto a piece of white paper and label it "wrist."

5. Make prints of your elbow or knee, knuckles, and nose. You may need to make more pencil markings on the paper before you make a new print.

6. Then clean your skin with soap and water to get off all the pencil markings.

7. Do all of the prints look the same? Describe them.

_____

_____

_____

Activity 4: Dirty Window

1. Find a window near you that you can see into.

2. Press your hands and face against the window. Hold them there for a few seconds.

3. Back up and look closely at the window. What does the window look like now? Why do you think this happened? Don't forget to clean the window when you are done!

_____

_____

_____

You have learned a lot about your skin! Think back to your four activities. Describe what you learned about the skin by doing them.

_____

_____

_____

_____

Student Guide

Optional: More on Skin and Skin Protection

The skin helps protect the systems of our body, but we need to protect our skin, too! Learn about the structures of the skin and what we need to do to protect it.

Lesson Objectives

- Identify *melanin* as the substance in skin that determines color.
- Label structures of the skin: sweat glands, hair follicles, oil glands, and sense receptors.
- List ways to care for and protect skin.

PREPARE

Approximate lesson time is 60 minutes.

Materials

For the Student

> Layers of Skin
> Sunscreen

Keywords and Pronunciation

chlorophyll (KLOR-uh-fil)

epidermis (eh-puh-DUR-muhs)**:** The outermost skin layer. The epidermis is the layer of skin that you can see.

hair follicle: The part of the skin that contains the root of a hair. The follicle is made of cells originally from the epidermis, but is mostly in the dermis. Each hair on your head grows out of a tiny hair follicle.

melanin (MEH-luh-nuhn)**:** A pigment found in skin and hair that gives them color. When skin is exposed to sun, it makes more melanin.

oil gland: A gland that opens into the hair follicle to reach the skin surface. The oil from the gland, called sebum, helps keep skin and hair from drying out. Our oil glands help keep skin protected.

photosynthesis (foh-toh-SINT-thuh-suhs)

sense receptors: Parts of the skin that allow feeling. Skin has four main types of sense receptors: for cold, heat, pressure, and pain. Thanks to sense receptors for heat, I could tell that the oven was still on.

sweat gland: A gland that leads to a small opening, called a *pore,* on the skin's surface. Sweat, or perspiration, is the liquid released through the pore. Sweat glands help us cool off.

LEARN

Activity 1: Optional: Lesson Instructions (*Online*)

Activity 2: Optional: Know and Protect Your Skin (*Online*)

Activity 3: Optional: Layers of Skin (*Online*)

Activity 4: Optional: Sunscreen (*Offline*)

Overview

Plants, like our skin, need sunlight and are affected by it. *Chlorophyll*, a substance inside the cells of plants, uses the sun to make energy for the plant. We call this process *photosynthesis*. If you look at a plant and notice places where it is green, you are looking at chlorophyll. What happens to a plant's leaves when the light is blocked? Can we use a plant to demonstrate an effect of sunscreen? Find a plant and discover for yourself.

Activity Steps

1. Cut a square of construction paper 3 cm x 3 cm.

2. Using a paper clip, carefully attach the square to cover about 1/3 of a leaf of a plant, preferably one with large leaves.

3. Apply the sunscreen to about 1/2 the uncovered part of the leaf.

4. Place the entire plant under a lamp, no more than 30 cm away from the bulb. Leave the light on throughout the experiment. You'll want to keep the plant well watered also.

5. After 24 hours, remove the paper and observe the leaves. What do you notice? Explain in your own words what happened to the leaves. You may use the Explore to help with your explanation.

6. Place the paper back on the leaf in the same place. Reapply sunscreen on the leaf in the same spot.

7. Continue the steps for three days.

   Note: *This activity is most effective when using sunscreen containing SPF 30 or higher.*

Conclusion

You may have noticed that when a plant does not get enough sun, the leaves start to turn a paler green. The leaf is protected from the sun. Our skin gets protection from the sun when we use sunscreen. Our skin's pigment, melanin, causes our skin to turn darker from the sun exposure, just like the chlorophyll causes the plant leaf to get a darker green. Remember though, that a plant needs sun for energy. Our skin doesn't need the sun to make energy for our bodies. So let the sun shine on plants, but protect your skin from it!

Name_____   Date_____

More on Skin and Skin Protection
Layers of Skin

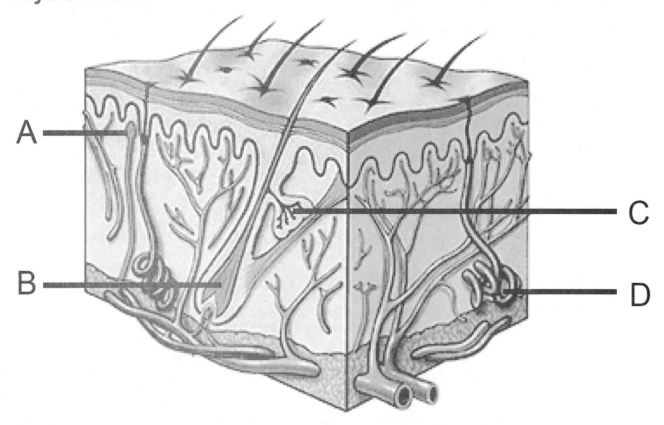

Each structure of the skin has a job to do.

Below, name the structure labeled and describe the function of each one.

   A.

   (a) Name:_____

   (b) Function:

_____

_____

_____

B.

   (a) Name:_____

   (b) Function:

_____

_____

_____

C.

   (a) Name: _____

   (b) Function:

_____

_____

_____

D.

   (a) Name:_____

   (b) Function:

_____

_____

_____

Name _____ Date _____

More on Skin and Skin Protection
Sunscreen

Overview

Plants, like our skin, need sunlight and are affected by it. Chlorophyll, a substance inside the cells of plants, uses the sun to make energy for the plant. We call this process photosynthesis. If you look at a plant and notice places where it is green, you are looking at chlorophyll. What happens to a plant's leaves when the light is blocked? Can we use a plant to demonstrate an effect of sunscreen? Find a plant and discover for yourself.

Activity Steps

1. Cut a square of construction paper, 3cm x 3cm.

2. Using a paper clip, carefully attach the square to cover about 1/3 of a leaf of a plant, preferably one with large leaves.

3. Apply sunscreen to about 1/2 the uncovered part of the leaf.

4. Place the plant under a lamp as close as possible. Leave the light on throughout the experiment.

5. After 24 hours, remove the paper and observe the leaves. What do you notice? Explain in your own words what happened to the leaves. You may use the Explore to help with your explanation.

   _____

   _____

   _____

   _____

6. Place the paper back on the leaf in the same place. Reapply sunscreen on the leaf in the same spot.

7. Continue the steps for 3 days.

Student Guide

Human Body: Unit Review and Assessment

Review and test your knowledge of everything you have learned about the skeleton, muscles, and skin of the human body—from identifying different types of skeleton bones to explaining the structure and function of your body's largest organ—your skin!

Lesson Objectives

- Demonstrate mastery of the knowledge and skills taught in this unit.
- Explain that bones, cartilage, tendons, and ligaments make up the skeletal system.
- Explain the main functions of the skin (protecting against infection, helping keep the body's internal temperature constant, and sensing the environment).
- Recognize that cells form tissues, tissues form organs, organs form body systems, and systems work together to make up the human body.
- Recognize that *voluntary muscles* are muscles you can move when you want to, while *involuntary muscles* are muscles that move automatically.
- State that most skeletal muscles work in pairs.
- Classify bones by function: support, protection, or movement.
- Demonstrate mastery of the important knowledge and skills taught in this unit.
- Describe how bones and muscles interact to cause movement.
- Explain that *flexor muscles* contract to bend joints as *extensor muscles* relax, and *extensor* muscles contract to straighten joints as *flexors* relax.
- Explain that red marrow forms blood cells and is located in the cavities of spongy bone.
- Explain the function of the skeletal, smooth, and cardiac muscles.
- Identify five of the many bones of the skeletal system.
- Identify the skin as the body's largest organ.
- Identify the three types of muscles (skeletal, smooth, and cardiac).
- Identify the two main layers of the skin as the epidermis and dermis and explain their main characteristics.
- Label structures of the skin: sweat glands, hair follicles, oil glands, and sense receptors.
- Recognize that bones are made up of various types of cells, blood vessels, nerves, and minerals like calcium.
- Recognize that hair and nails are part of the skin system.

PREPARE

Approximate lesson time is 60 minutes.

LEARN

Activity 1: Human Body Unit Review *(Online)*

ASSESS

Unit Assessment: Human Body *(Online)*

You will complete an online Unit Assessment covering the main objectives of the unit.

Student Guide

Introduction to Vertebrates: Fish

A backbone gives many animals a place to hang their muscles and organs. Animals can be classified according to whether or not they have a backbone. A vertebrate is an animal with a backbone. Fish are a type of vertebrate that are distinguished by their jaws and skeleton.

Lesson Objectives

- Identify different groups of vertebrates (fish, amphibians, reptiles, birds, and mammals) according to their common characteristics.
- Distinguish between *vertebrates* and *invertebrates.*
- Recognize that some animals have a constant internal body temperature and others have an internal temperature that fluctuates depending on the temperature of the surroundings.
- Distinguish between vertebrates that maintain a constant internal body temperature and those that do not.
- Explain the difference between a *vertebrate* and an *invertebrate.*
- Describe some characteristics of jawless fish, cartilaginous fish, and bony fish.
- Identify the key parts of most fish: gills, scales, and fins.

PREPARE

Approximate lesson time is 60 minutes.

Advance Preparation

- If you plan to do the optional activity, which involves dissecting a fish, you will need to buy a fish from a fish market or grocery store. Make sure the internal organs are intact (the fish should not be gutted). You may wish to take a picture of your student performing this dissection. If so, be sure that you have a camera and film available.
- If you plan to do the optional activity, which involves dissecting a fish, you will need to buy a fish from a fish market or grocery store. Make sure the internal organs are intact (the fish should not be gutted). You may wish to take a picture of your student performing this dissection. If so, be sure that you have a camera available.

Materials

For the Student

    Bodies, Fins, and Tails

Keywords and Pronunciation

cartilage (KAHR-tl-ij)**:** Strong, flexible tissue that forms the skeleton of some fish. A shark's skeleton is not hard and bony, but is made of flexible cartilage.

cartilaginous (kahr-tuh-LA-juh-nuhs)

gills: The breathing organs of a fish and of most other animals that live in the water. Gills remove oxygen from the water and release carbon dioxide, allowing the fish to "breathe" underwater.

invertebrate: An animal with no backbone. Squid, worms, and insects are invertebrates.

plankton: Plants or animals that float or drift in the water. Plankton can take the form of microscopic plants and animals or much larger organisms such as shrimp-like krill and jellyfish.

predator: An animal that hunts and eats other animals. Sharks are ocean predators.

vertebrae (VUR-tuh-bray)**:** The small bones that make up the backbone. The bumps you feel in your back are your vertebrae.

vertebrate (VUR-tuh-bruht)**:** An animal that has a backbone. Cats are vertebrates, but worms are not.

LEARN

Activity 1: Who Has a Backbone? *(Online)*

Safety

As usual, you will want to preview any websites and recommended reading materials listed here before having your student view them.

Activity 2: The Three Types of Fish *(Offline)*

Activity 3: Bodies, Fins, and Tails *(Offline)*

ASSESS

Lesson Assessment: Introduction to Vertebrates: Fish *(Offline)*

Sit with an adult to review the assessment questions.

LEARN

Activity 4: Internal Anatomy of a Fish *(Offline)*

Name _____   Date _____

Introduction to Vertebrates: Fish

Bodies, Fins, and Tails

Fish use pectoral fins to steer, brake, back up, and move up and down. Fish use their caudal fins and tails to propel themselves forward. You can make predictions about how fast a fish will move just by looking at its body shape, pectoral fins, and caudal fin.

Body Shapes

Ray: A flat body from top to bottom is good for hiding on the sea floor.

Moray eel: A long, slender body is good for hiding under rocks.

Coral reef fish: A flat body from side to side fits into tight spots. These fish often look roundish from the side.

Tuna: A streamlined body of a fast swimmer that does not need to hide

Fins

Long and pointed pectoral fin

Crescent-shaped caudal fin

Tuna: Fast swimmer! Streamlined body

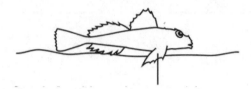

Sculpin: Has short, stubby pectoral fins for "walking" on the bottom of the sea floor

Round pectoral fin

Flat caudal fin, not "V" notched or crescent

Snapper: A medium swimmer, round pectoral fins for moving side to side

Fan shaped caudal fin

Flowing pectoral fins

Lionfish: Slow swimmer

Cut out the body shapes, pectoral fins, and caudal fins and use them to build different fish. Then tell whether your fish swim quickly or slowly and where they might hide in the water, if they hide at all!

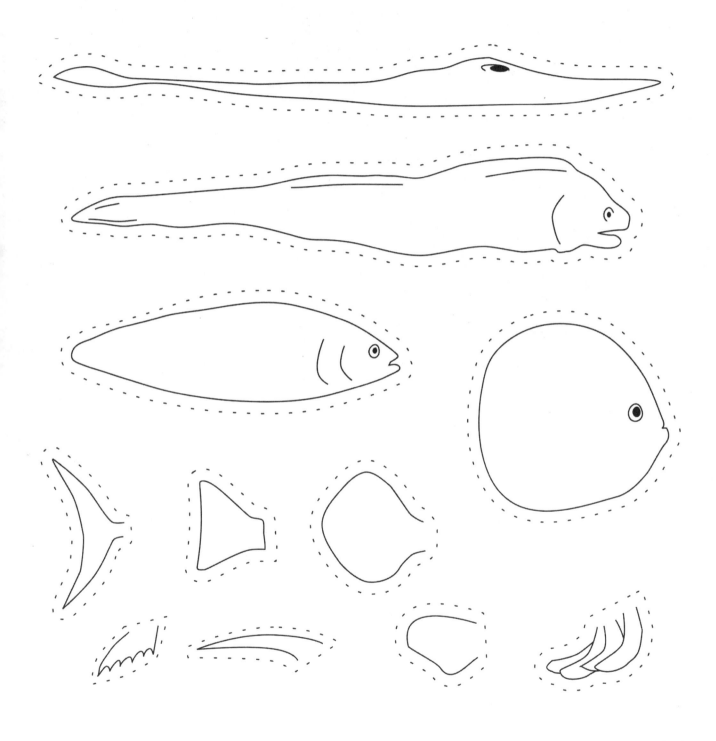

Student Guide

Amphibians and Reptiles

Amphibians and reptiles are both vertebrates, but they are different in many ways. How can you tell them apart? Learn the characteristics of amphibians and reptiles, and find out how a legless, gilled tadpole becomes a hopping adult frog.

Lesson Objectives

- Describe some characteristics of amphibians.
- Describe some characteristics of reptiles.
- Describe the metamorphosis of a frog from tadpole to adult.

PREPARE

Approximate lesson time is 60 minutes.

Advance Preparation

- If you choose to do the optional activity and observe the metamorphosis of a frog, you'll need to obtain frog eggs or tadpoles. If you live near a pond or lake, you can collect eggs or tadpoles there in early spring.
- You can also order tadpoles from a biological supply house, a local pet store, or through the Internet. Some suppliers provide kits that include the aquarium, tadpoles, food, and instructions for raising tadpoles. The best time to place your order is early spring. Suppliers, however, often have tadpoles available throughout much of the year. The frog *Xenopus laevis* is a good species to raise, as it develops more rapidly than many others.
- If you plan to raise a tadpole without using a kit, visit the *Frogland* site to learn how.
- If you choose to do the optional activity and observe the metamorphosis of a frog, you'll need to obtain frog eggs or tadpoles. If you live near a pond or lake, you can collect eggs or tadpoles there in early spring.
- You can also order tadpoles from a biological supply house, a local pet store, or through the Internet. Some suppliers provide kits that include the aquarium, tadpoles, food, and instructions for raising tadpoles. The best time to place your order is early spring. Suppliers, however, often have tadpoles available throughout much of the year. The frog *Xenopus laevis* is a good species to raise, as it develops more rapidly than many others.
- If you plan to raise a tadpole without using a kit, visit the *Frogland* site to learn how.

Materials

For the Student

    Frogs and Toads

Keywords and Pronunciation

amphibian (am-FIH-bee-uhn)**:** A vertebrate that spends part of its life in water and part of its life on land. Frogs, toads, and salamanders are amphibians.

herpetology (hur-puh-TAH-luh-jee)

metamorphosis (meh-tuh-MOR-fuh-suhs)**:** The process that takes place as a young organism changes in appearance and becomes an adult. Metamorphosis occurs when a caterpillar becomes a butterfly.

reptile: A vertebrate that has dry, scaly skin and lays tough, leathery eggs. Crocodiles, turtles, and snakes are reptiles.

tadpole: A frog or toad in the gilled, legless stage of its life cycle, just after it hatches from its egg. Also called a pollywog. Down by the lake, we saw hundreds of tadpoles swimming in the water.

vertebrate (VUR-tuh-bruht)

LEARN

Activity 1: Be a Herpetologist *(Online)*

Activity 2: Frogs and Toads *(Offline)*

ASSESS

Lesson Assessment: Amphibians and Reptiles *(Offline)*

Sit with an adult to review the assessment questions.

LEARN

Activity 3: Raise a Tadpole *(Offline)*

Name _____ Date _____

Amphibians and Reptiles

Frogs and Toads

Frogs and toads are both amphibians. They spend part of their lives in water and part of their lives on land. Adult frogs live near moist areas. Adult toads can be found in drier places. Study the pictures of the frog and toad and then follow the directions.

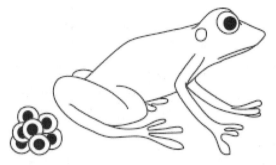 

1. Frogs have bulging eyes that allow the frog to poke its eyes above the water's surface and have an above-water view while nearly all the rest of its body remains safely underwater. Color the frog's eyes. Draw an insect nearby for it to see.

2. Toads have glands behind their eyes that contain poison. The poison is not very appetizing to animals that want to eat toads! Color the poison glands behind the toad's eyes.

3. Toads have dry, bumpy skin. Draw a few more bumps on the toad.

4. Frogs have smooth, moist skin. Color the frog's skin so it looks smooth.

5. A frog's long, muscular legs are built for long jumps and fast swims. Draw a lily pad for the frog.

6. A toad's legs are short for short hops. Draw the ground for the toad to hop on.

7. Frogs lay eggs in groups. Toads lay eggs in long chains. Draw more eggs near the frog and the toad.

8. Frogs have webbed feet. Toads usually have no or very little webbing between their toes. Draw the webbing on the frog's back feet.

9. Frogs sense sound through a circular membrane that is located right behind their eyes. Sound waves traveling through the air or water cause this membrane to vibrate back and forth, sending a signal to the frog's brain. Color the frog's "ear" light green.

Student Guide

Birds

Birds are vertebrates that can fly. What gives birds the ability to soar through the air? A bird's body is specially adapted for flying. Learn about these special adaptations for flight. Then see how one adaptation, the gizzard, helps give a bird the energy it needs to fly high in the sky.

Lesson Objectives

- Describe the functions of the crop and the gizzard.
- Identify structures in birds' bodies that help birds fly.
- Name two characteristics of birds that make birds different from reptiles.

PREPARE

Approximate lesson time is 60 minutes.

Materials

For the Student

> Why Birds Can Fly

Keywords and Pronunciation

crop: The part of a bird's digestive system that stores and continuously releases food to provide energy for the bird to fly. As the robin swallowed worm after worm, it stored them in its crop.

gizzard: An organ in a bird's digestive system that grinds food so the bird can digest the food more easily. Many birds swallow sand or small pebbles to help the gizzard grind the food. A bird's gizzard will crush seeds, insects, worms, and nuts into smaller pieces.

LEARN

Activity 1: It's for the Birds *(Online)*

Safety

As usual, you will want to preview any websites listed here before having your student view them.

Activity 2: Structures for Flight *(Offline)*

Activity 3: The Grinding Gizzard *(Offline)*

Instructions

body { font-family: Arial, Verdana, sans-serif; background-color: white; }

What do you think birds eat? Birds may eat seeds, insects, fruits, nuts, or worms. When birds eat, they sometimes swallow sand or tiny pebbles along with their food. These pebbles are important for a bird's digestion.

Birds must digest food quickly so they have enough energy to fly. Birds have a special organ in their digestive system called a gizzard, which grinds up their food so the bird can digest it more easily. Many birds swallow sand or small pebbles to help grind their food. Try this activity to see how a bird's gizzard grinds food:

1. Prepare

Use a zipper-close plastic bag to represent the gizzard. Fill the bottom of the bag with tiny pebbles.

2. Fill

Place any of the following "bird food" into the bag:

- popped popcorn and/or rice to represent insects nuts or seeds to represent seeds piece of bread to represent a mouse grapes to represent fruit gummy worms and dry oatmeal to represent worms and mud

3. Seal

Press the air out of the bag and seal it.

4. Grind

Grind the tiny pebbles and bird food together. Notice how the pieces of food become smaller. Small pieces of food are easier to digest than large pieces

ASSESS

Lesson Assessment: Birds *(Offline)*

Sit with an adult to review the assessment questions.

Name _____   Date _____

Birds

Why Birds Can Fly

Birds have special adaptations that help them fly. Write down how each part of a bird's body helps it fly. Then color the bird.

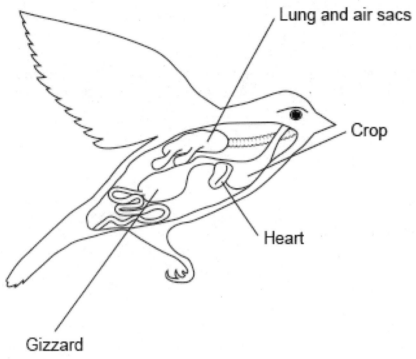

Lung and air sacs

_____

_____

Crop

_____

_____

Heart

_____

_____

Gizzard

_____

_____

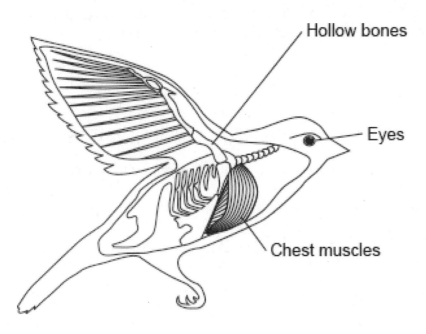

Hollow bones

_____

_____

Eyes

_____

_____

Chest muscles

_____

_____

Student Guide
Mammals

What is a mammal? Mammals are the only vertebrates that have hair at some time in their lives and that produce milk in mammary glands. Learn the different ways mammals give birth to their young, and how mammals use their molars, canines, and incisors to eat.

Lesson Objectives

- Identify and describe the functions of incisors, molars, and canines.
- Identify the characteristics all mammals have in common (for example, hair, the ability to produce milk from mammary glands, a constant internal body temperature, and being vertebrates).
- Identify the three ways mammals have their young: born live, born into a pouch, and hatched from an egg.
- Use information from informational text to argue that some animals form groups that help members survive.

PREPARE

Approximate lesson time is 60 minutes.

Materials

For the Student

Teeth Tell All

Keywords and Pronunciation

canines: Long, pointed teeth mammals use to stab and tear prey. The leopard used its sharp canines to grab the gazelle and carry the animal up the tree.

carnivore (KAHR-nuh-vor)**:** An animal that feeds mainly on other animals. A tiger is considered a carnivore since its diet is mainly other animals.

echidna (ih-KID-nuh)

herbivore (UR-buh-vor)**:** An animal that feeds mainly on plants. A cow is considered an herbivore since its diet is mainly plants.

incisor (in-SIY-zur)

incisors: Chisel-shaped front teeth that animals use for cutting and gnawing. When you bite into an apple, you cut and tear a piece off with your eight incisors.

limb: An animal's arm, leg, or wing, or flipper. Dolphins' limbs are adapted for swimming.

mammal: A vertebrate that has hair at some point in its life and mammary glands that produce milk to feed its young. Cats, dogs, cows, dolphins, and sea lions are all mammals.

mammary gland: A part of a female mammal's body that produces milk for her young. A calf receives vitamins, minerals, and protein from milk produced in its mother's mammary glands.

marsupial (mahr-SOO-pee-uhl)

molars: Broad, flat teeth, located behind the incisors and canines that are good for grinding. Elephants and horses use their large molars to grind up the plants they eat.

omnivore (AHM-nih-vor)**:** An animal that eats both plants and animals. Bears are omnivores, and eat fruits and nuts as well as fish and other small animals.

platypus (PLA-tih-puhs)

LEARN

Activity 1: I Am a Mammal *(Online)*

Activity 2: Teeth Tell All *(Offline)*

Activity 3: Animals Form Groups *(Online)*

Select the Explore button to begin. Read the Big Universe books *A Flock of Sheep* by Alex Kuskowski, *A Herd of Deer, Animal Groups in the Forest* by Alex Kuskowski, and *A Gaggle of Geese, Animal Groups on Lakes and Rivers* by Alex Kuskowski. Answer questions at the end of each book to check understanding.

ASSESS

Lesson Assessment: Mammals *(Online)*

You will complete an online assessment covering the main objectives of the lesson.

LEARN

Activity 4: Visit the San Diego Zoo *(Online)*

Safety

As usual, you may wish to preview any websites listed here before your student views them.

Name _____   Date _____

Mammals

Teeth Tell All

Did you know that by looking at a mammal's teeth you can tell what kinds of food the animal eats? *Herbivores* eat only plants and have broad, flat molars for chewing and grinding. *Carnivores* eat only animals and have large incisors for cutting and long, sharp canines for stabbing and tearing their food. *Omnivores* eat both animals and plants. They have molars, incisors, and canines.

Study the teeth of each mammal. Then answer the questions.

1. Write the function of each type of tooth on the lines provided.

2. Look closely at each set of teeth, and remember to look at all the different types of teeth.

   (a) Write *herbivore* on the line near the mammal that eats only plants.

   (b) How can you tell that mammal is an herbivore?

   _____

   _____

   (c) Write *carnivore* on the line near the mammal that is a meat-eater.

   (d) How can you tell that mammal is a carnivore?

   _____

   _____

   (e) Write *omnivore* on the line near the mammal that eats both plants and animals.

   (f) How can you tell that mammal is an omnivore?

   _____

   _____

3. Explain why looking at a mammal's teeth helps you find out what it might eat.

_____

_____

_____

_____

_____

_____

Incisors

_____

Canines

_____

Molars

_____

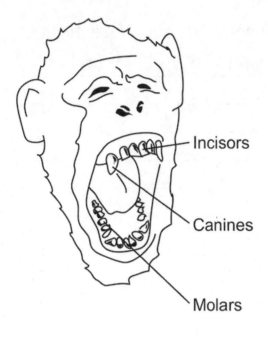

Incisors

_____

Canines

_____

Molars

_____

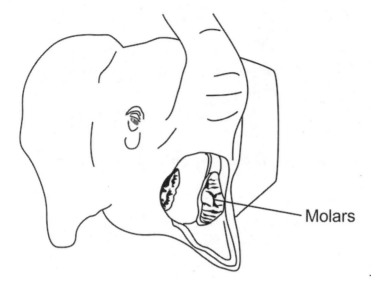

Molars

Molars

_____

_____

Student Guide

Classification of Vertebrates: Unit Review and Assessment

Review and demonstrate what you've learned about vertebrates.

Lesson Objectives

- Identify different groups of vertebrates (fish, amphibians, reptiles, birds, and mammals) according to their common characteristics.
- Distinguish between *vertebrates* and *invertebrates.*
- Recognize that some animals have a constant internal body temperature and others have an internal temperature that fluctuates depending on the temperature of the surroundings.
- Explain the difference between a *vertebrate* and an *invertebrate.*
- Describe some characteristics of amphibians.
- Describe some characteristics of reptiles.
- Describe the metamorphosis of a frog from tadpole to adult.
- Identify and describe the functions of incisors, molars, and canines.
- Identify structures in birds' bodies that help birds fly.
- Identify the characteristics all mammals have in common (for example, hair, the ability to produce milk from mammary glands, a constant internal body temperature, and are vertebrates).
- Identify the three ways mammals have their young: born live, born into a pouch, and hatched from an egg.
- Name two characteristics of birds that make birds different from reptiles.

PREPARE

Approximate lesson time is 60 minutes.

Keywords and Pronunciation

metamorphosis (meh-tuh-MOR-fuh-suhs)**:** The process that takes place as a young organism changes in appearance and becomes an adult. Metamorphosis occurs when a caterpillar becomes a butterfly.

LEARN

Activity 1: Classification of Vertebrates *(Online)*

ASSESS

Unit Assessment: Classification of Vertebrates *(Offline)*

Complete an offline Unit Assessment. Your learning coach will score the assessment.

Student Guide

What's an Ecosystem?

Learn how scientists use patterns of climate, vegetation, and animal life to identify ecosystems. Travel around the world to discover the different climate zones and the ecosystems within them.

Lesson Objectives

- Explain that an *ecosystem* includes all living and nonliving things that interact in a particular region.
- Recognize that living things have both physical and behavioral adaptations that enable them to survive in a particular ecosystem.
- Define *climate* as the usual weather pattern in a certain area over many years.
- Describe different ecosystems (tundra, boreal forest, deciduous forest, tropical rain forest, grasslands, desert, freshwater, and marine).
- Identify the three main climate zones as tropical, temperate, and polar.
- Recognize that scientists use patterns of climate, vegetation, and animal life to identify different ecosystems.
- Recognize that scientists identify different ecosystems by studying their patterns of climate, vegetation, and animal life.
- Define *climate* as the usual weather in a certain area over many years.

PREPARE

Approximate lesson time is 60 minutes.

Materials

For the Student

Climates Around the World

Keywords and Pronunciation

adaptation (a-dap-TAY-shuhn): A change in a body part or behavior that makes an organism better able to survive in its surroundings. Heavy fur is an adaptation that enables some animals to live in very cold climates.

boreal (BOR-ee-uhl)

climate: The usual pattern of weather that has occurred in an area over a long period of time. California's climate consists of hot, dry summers and mild, rainy winters.

ecology: The study of how animals and plants interact with their surroundings.

ecosystem (EE-koh-sis-tuhm): A community or group of organisms living and interacting with each other and their environment.

environment (in-VIY-ruhn-muhnt): The part of an ecosystem that includes all the nonliving and living factors that affect an organism. The wind, water, soil, and interactions with other animals are all part of a rabbit's environment.

polar zone: Parts of the Earth where the climate is extremely cold and dry. Polar zones are located near the North and South Poles.

precipitation: Water that falls from clouds as rain, hail, snow, or sleet. A weather map shows areas that are receiving precipitation.

temperate zone: The parts of the Earth located between the tropical zones near the equator, and the polar zones near the North and South Poles. The climate of a temperate zone is generally cold in the winter, warm in the summer, and moderate during the spring and fall. Much of the United States is in the temperate zone.

tropical zone: The part of the Earth near the equator, where the weather is warm or hot all year long. Many people go on vacations in the tropical zone.

tundra (TUN-druh)

LEARN

Activity 1: Ecosystems (Online)

Safety

As usual, you will want to preview any websites or recommended reading materials before having your student view them.

Activity 2: Climates Around the World (Offline)

Complete the Climates Around the World activity sheet to review climates and ecosystems. Save the sheet for future lessons.

ASSESS

Lesson Assessment: What's an Ecosystem? (Offline)

Sit with an adult to review the assessment questions.

LEARN

Activity 3: The Greenhouse Effect (Offline)

You have learned that the types of plants and animals that live in an ecosystem depend on the climate of the ecosystem. The Earth's climate has a lot to do with the temperature of the air. But what heats the air?

Energy from the sun passes through the Earth's atmosphere. Some of this energy bounces back into space, but most of it changes to heat as it warms the Earth's surface. Instead of just flying back out into space, this heat energy gets trapped by gases in the atmosphere and heats up the air.

This heating process is called the greenhouse effect after the greenhouses people use for raising plants that need bright, warm conditions. The Earth's atmosphere acts like the panes of glass in a greenhouse. The glass lets sunlight pass through, but does not allow heat to escape. The air inside a greenhouse gets warmer than the air outside.

The same thing happens all over Earth. Without our atmosphere, all the heat bouncing off the Earth's surface would escape into space, and the Earth's surface would freeze. The greenhouse effect keeps our air nice and warm.

1. Investigate

Place the two thermometers in direct sunlight or under a bright lamp.

2. Record

Wait 5 minutes to allow the thermometers to warm up, then record the temperature of both.

3. Make a Chart

While you are waiting, make a chart to record your measurements.

Make three equal columns on a piece of lined paper.

Write the following headings at the top of the paper: Time, Thermometer No. 1, Thermometer No. 2 (jar).

Write the numbers 1-10 under the Time heading. You will be taking a total of 10 temperature measurements.

4. Place

After you have taken your first measurement, place the jar over one of the thermometers. Make sure the jar does not cast a shadow over the second thermometer.

5. Record

Record the temperature every minute for 10 minutes.

Conclude

Refer to your data chart. How did the air temperature over each thermometer change? Why do you think the temperature of the air *inside* the jar increased, compared to the air temperature *outside* the jar? [1] How is this process similar to the greenhouse effect that warms the Earth's atmosphere? [2]

Name _____ Date _____

What's an Ecosystem?
Climates Around the World

Define the following words:

1. climate

_____

2. ecosystem

_____

Use the World Climate Zone and World Ecosystems map in the Explore Activity to complete the following questions:

3. Locate and trace the following:

   (a) the Equator

   (b) the Arctic Circle

   (c) the Antarctic Circle

   (d) the Tropic of Cancer

   (e) the Tropic of Capricorn

4. Write the names of each climate zone on the map.

5. Use your map key to lightly color each climate zone on the map.

6. In the spaces below, describe the climate in each of the following regions:

   (a) tropical

   _____

   (b) temperate

   _____

   (c) polar

   _____

7. List at least one ecosystem that is found in each climate zone.

    (a) tropical

    _____

    (b) temperate

    _____

    (c) polar

    _____

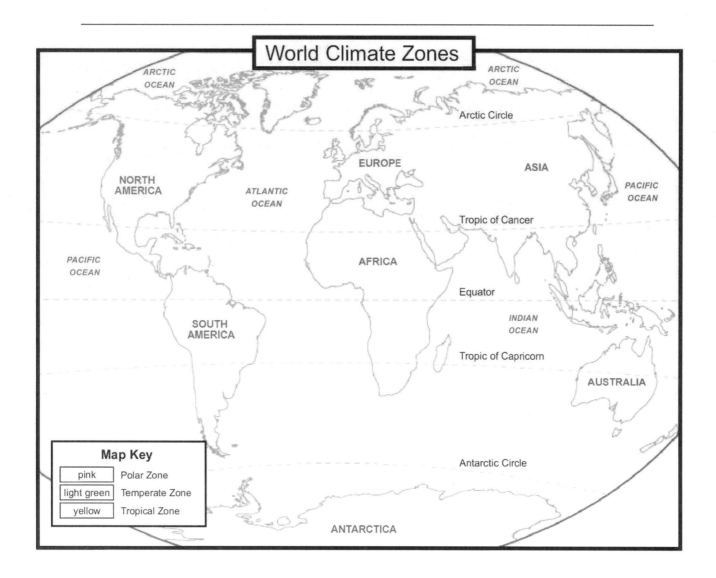

Student Guide

Tundra

Read *A Walk in the Tundra* to learn about the climate of the tundra and the plants and animals that live there.

Lesson Objectives

- Describe two adaptations of plants that live in the tundra (for example, the need to grow low to the ground to escape fierce winds).
- Identify and describe key characteristics of the tundra (for example, a cold, dry, and harsh climate).
- Describe two adaptations of animals that live in the tundra (for example, the ability to hibernate through the winter, and hoof shapes that keep the animal from sinking in the snow).
- Identify two animals that live in the tundra (for example, caribou, geese, and arctic foxes).
- Identify two plants that live in the tundra (for example, mosses, grasses, and wildflowers).

PREPARE

Approximate lesson time is 60 minutes.

Materials

For the Student

> Reading Guide
> Tundra Research
> *A Walk in the Tundra* by Rebecca L. Johnson

Keywords and Pronunciation

adaptation (a-dap-TAY-shuhn)**:** A change in a body part or behavior that makes an organism better able to survive in its surroundings.

biome (BIY-ohm)**:** A large area with a distinctive community of animals and plants that live in an area with a similar climate. The tundra is a biome that covers a large area of the northern part of all the continents in the northern hemisphere.

hibernate: To spend the winter in an inactive, or dormant, state. Woodchucks and frogs hibernate all winter long, but bears do not. Bears often wake up and roam about during warm winter days.

permafrost: Permanently frozen ground beneath the top layer of soil. Most tundra plants have shallow roots because their roots cannot grow down through the layer of permafrost.

tundra (TUN-druh)

LEARN

Activity 1: A Walk in the Tundra *(Online)*

Select the Explore button to begin. Print the Reading Guide when you are ready to read.

Safety

As usual, you will want to preview any websites or recommended reading materials before having your student view them.

Activity 2: Tundra Research *(Offline)*

Use the book to complete the Tundra Research activity sheet.

ASSESS

Lesson Assessment: Tundra *(Offline)*

Sit with an adult to review the assessment questions.

LEARN

Activity 3: Blubber *(Offline)*

Blubber Keeps Animals Warm

Many animals that live in polar climates—such as polar bears, walruses, and whales—have a thick layer of fat, or *blubber,* to protect them from the cold. Blubber helps these animals stay warm by insulating them from the cold and helping them maintain a constant body temperature.

An *insulator* is a material that allows little or no energy (in this case heat) to pass through it. What does this mean to an animal with a thick layer of insulating blubber? The blubber helps the animal hold in its body heat and keep out the cold!

This activity will demonstrate how fat can insulate against the cold.

Investigate

1. Fill one coffee mug with shortening or lard and leave the other mug empty.

2. Make a hole in the center of each cardboard square. The holes should be small enough to hold the thermometers snugly.

3. Place the cardboard squares over the mugs and position the thermometers in the holes so the bulbs extend into the mug. Make sure the bulbs do not touch the bottoms or the sides of the mugs.

4. Let the cups sit until they are both at room temperature. Record the temperature.

5. Place both mugs into the refrigerator. If it is cold outside, you may wish to place the mugs outside.

6. Record the temperature on both thermometers after 10, 20, and 30 minutes.

Conclude

Which mug cooled more slowly? [1]

How does this experiment represent how blubber keeps animals warm? [2]

Extension

Repeat the experiment starting with cold mugs, and allow the mugs to warm to room temperature. Compare the amount of time it takes for both mugs to warm up from identical cold temperatures to room temperatures. Which mug would you expect to take longer to warm up? [3] Why? [4]

Hint: Remember that fat is a good insulator, and helps block the flow of heat from one place to another.

Activity 4: Optional: Where Does the Water Go? (*Offline*)

Permafrost

If you were to dig a hole in the tundra, the first 30 cm (12 inches) of soil would be fairly easy to move. Then you would hit what felt like solid rock. This hard layer is actually permafrost—soil that is permanently frozen. Permafrost keeps melting snow water from soaking any deeper into the ground.

Investigate to see what happens in the spring when the winter snow that covers the tundra begins to melt.

Investigate

1. Prepare some gelatin dessert; half-fill a clear plastic container with the gelatin and refrigerate.

2. When the gelatin is set, smooth a layer of chocolate ice cream over the top followed by a layer of vanilla ice cream. The chocolate ice cream represents the upper layer of soil that freezes only during the winter. The vanilla ice cream is the snow, and the gelatin is the permafrost.

3. Watch what happens when the ice cream melts.

Conclude

Does the ice cream melt down into the gelatin layer? [1]

What do you think might happen in the tundra once the snow melts in the spring? [2]

Name _____   Date _____

Tundra
Reading Guide

Using the Reading Guide

Today you will read *A Walk in the Tundra* by Rebecca L. Johnson. This lesson is the first of six lessons in the book series. All six books follow the same general format. At the beginning of each book is a section called Words to Know. This is a glossary with definitions and pronunciations of words in the book. You may find it useful to review these words before you begin reading.

On page 8 of the book is a map of North America, color-coded to show the different ecosystems (or biomes). Begin by having your student point to the region that is the focus of that lesson.

Introduction to Research

Your student will learn about research and note taking by completing a list and answering some questions about each ecosystem. Encourage your student to search the reading for accurate responses and write them in the correct spaces on the list.

Remind your student that taking notes is different from most other types of writing. Notes don't necessarily have to be in complete sentences. Sometimes a simple list is the best way to organize information.

Use the sample list provided to guide your student's reading and note taking. When completing the list, it is not necessary for your student to list all possible answers.

Name of ecosystem (or biome):

- Tundra

Climate (temperate, polar, or tropical):

- Polar

Climate description (page 10):

- Cold, icy, windy, dry

Geographic location (pages 6–8):

- Northern part of all the continents at the top of the world
- In North America, from the Arctic Ocean south to the middle of Canada

Types of plants (pages 18–24):

- Mosses
- Grasses
- Wildflowers
- Small shrubs
- Lichens (Lichens are not true plants, but are fungi that live in close association with algae or bacteria.)

Plant adaptations (pages 18, 19, 21):

- Grow low to the ground to escape fierce winds
- Shallow roots. Longer roots would be unable to grow into the permafrost.
- Stems and leaves covered in tiny hairs to keep from drying out
- Small, leathery leaves, capable of withstanding the wind and cold temperatures more effectively than large leaves

Types of animals (pages 24–45):

- Mice
- Lemmings
- Arctic hares
- Arctic foxes
-
- Polar bears
- Musk oxen
- Caribou
- Birds: ptarmigan, snowy owls, geese, loons

Animal adaptations (pages 26, 27, 28, 34, 43, 44):

- For the arctic hare and the arctic fox, fur coloration helps the animal blend in with its background. Their fur is grayish-brown in summer, white in winter.
- The fox's fur has two layers: the soft, fluffy under-fur keeps in heat, while the thick guard hairs block the wind.
- Caribou hooves are shaped to keep them from sinking in the snow.
- Ptarmigans puff their feathers against the cold wind to stay warm.
- Some animals sleep all through winter in underground burrows or dens. This is known as hibernation.
- Musk oxen, foxes, and polar bears depend on thick layers of fat, called blubber, to get through the winter.

Name _____   Date _____

Tundra

Tundra Research

Use *A Walk in the Tundra* to fill in the information and answer the questions below. Page numbers have been provided to help you find the information in the book.

Name of ecosystem (or biome): _____

Climate (temperate, polar, or tropical): _____

Climate description (page 10):

_____

_____

_____

Geographic location (pages 6–8):

_____

Types of plants (pages 18–24):

_____

_____

_____

_____

Plant adaptations (pages 18, 19, 21):

_____

_____

_____

_____

_____

Types of animals (pages 24–45):

_____

_____

_____

_____

Animal adaptations (pages 26, 27, 28, 34, 43, 44):

_____

_____

_____

_____

_____

1. Describe two adaptations that help plants survive in the tundra.

_____

_____

_____

2. Describe two adaptations that help animals survive in the tundra.

_____

_____

_____

Student Guide

Boreal Forests

Read *A Walk in the Boreal Forest* to learn about the climate of the boreal forest and the plants and animals that live there.

Lesson Objectives

- Describe two adaptations of plants that live in the boreal forest (for example, conifer needles are covered with a waxy coating that keeps them from drying out).
- Identify and describe key characteristics of the boreal forest (for example, long, cold, snowy winters and short, warm summers).
- Describe two adaptations of animals that live in the boreal forest (for example, some animals hibernate to avoid the harsh winters).
- Identify two animals that live in the boreal forest (for example, moose, chipmunk, and woodpecker).
- Identify two plants that live in the boreal forest (for example, fir trees, wildflowers, and grasses).

PREPARE

Approximate lesson time is 60 minutes.

Materials

For the Student

> Reading Guide
> Boreal Forest Research
> *A Walk in the Boreal Forest* by Rebecca L. Johnson

Keywords and Pronunciation

adaptation (a-dap-TAY-shuhn)**:** A change in either the body structure or the behavior of an organism that makes it better able to survive in its environment.

biome (BIY-ohm)**:** A large area with a distinctive community of animals and plants that live in an area with a similar climate. The tundra is a biome that covers a large area of the northern part of all the continents in the northern hemisphere.

boreal (BOR-ee-uhl)

conifer (KAH-nuh-fur)

coniferous (kah-NIH-fuh-ruhs)

deciduous (dih-SIH-juh-wuhs)

hibernate: To spend the winter in an inactive, or dormant, state. Woodchucks and frogs hibernate all winter long, but bears do not. Bears often wake up and roam about during warm winter days.

photosynthesis (foh-toh-SINT-thuh-suhs)

stomata (STOH-muh-tuh)**:** Tiny openings in a leaf that allow gases to pass in and out. When the water in leaves evaporates, it escapes through the stomata.

taiga (TIY-guh)

LEARN

Activity 1: A Walk in the Boreal Forest *(Offline)*

Instructions

Use your book, A Walk in the Boreal Forest, to complete the Boreal Forest Research sheet. Page numbers on the sheet will help you find the information in the book.

Safety

As usual, you will want to preview any websites or recommended reading materials before having your student view them.

Activity 2: Boreal Forest Research *(Offline)*

Use your book, *A Walk in the Boreal Forest,* to complete the Boreal Forest Research sheet. Page numbers on the sheet will help you find the information in the book.

ASSESS

Lesson Assessment: Boreal Forests *(Offline)*

Sit with an adult to review the assessment questions.

LEARN

Activity 3: Optional: Deciduous and Coniferous Leaves *(Offline)*

Evaporation from Leaves

Leaves provide food for trees through a process called photosynthesis (foh-toh-SINT-thuh-suhs). During photosynthesis, leaves use carbon dioxide from the air, water absorbed from the ground through their roots, and energy from sunlight to make food for the tree. Leaves have small openings, called stomata (STOH-muh-tuh), that allow gases in and out. Trees also lose water through these holes.

The conifers in the boreal forest can withstand harsh winters because their leaves (needles) are small and have a waxy coating. The small leaf size and waxy coating help keep water from evaporating, or escaping through the leaves, and prevents the leaves from drying out in the cold winter wind.

Deciduous (dih-SIH-juh-wuhs) trees, such as oak and maple, have broad flat leaves with a large surface. This surface allows much more water to escape from the leaves. During the winter, water in the soil freezes and the tree roots cannot take in water to relace what is lost through the leaves. So, deciduous trees shed their leaves to keep from losing too much water through evaporation.

Compare the amount of water that evaporates from deciduous and coniferous (kah-NIH-fur-uhs) leaves.

Investigate

1. Get permission to cut two small branches, one from a coniferous (evergreen) tree and another from a deciduous tree. Make sure the branches are about the same size.

2. Place each branch in its own jar or tall glass of water.

3. Use a twist tie or string to secure a clear plastic bag around the needles of the coniferous branch, and another around the broad leaves of the deciduous branch.

4. Place both glasses in a sunny location for a few days. When water evaporates through the stomata on the leaves, the water will collect in the plastic bags.

5. From what you know about coniferous and deciduous leaves, hypothesize (provide a possible explanation) about which bag will collect more water. Write down your hypothesis and explain your reasons for thinking it is correct.

Conclude

Was your hypothesis correct? Why or why not?

Name _____ Date _____

Boreal Forests
Reading Guide

Using the Reading Guide

Read *A Walk in the Boreal Forest* by Rebecca L. Johnson. The Words to Know section at the beginning of the book is a glossary with definitions and pronunciations of words in the book. You may find it useful to review these words before you begin reading.

On page 8 of the book is a map of North America, color-coded to show the different ecosystems (or biomes). Begin by having your student point to the region that is the focus of the lesson.

Introduction to Research

Your student will learn about research and note taking by completing a list and answering some questions about each ecosystem. Encourage your student to search the reading for accurate responses and write them in the correct spaces on the list.

Remind your student that taking notes is different from most other types of writing. Notes don't necessarily have to be in complete sentences. Sometimes a simple list is the best way to organize information.

Use the sample list provided to guide your student's reading and note taking. When completing the list, it is not necessary for your student to list all possible answers.

Name of ecosystem (or biome):

- Boreal forest

Climate (temperate, polar, or tropical):

- Temperate

Climate description (page 10):

- Long, cold, and snowy winters and short, warm summers

Geographic locations (pages 6–8):

- Boreal forests stretch across the northern parts of North America, Europe, and Asia

Types of plants (pages 12–20, 39):

- Grasses
- Wildflowers
- Fir trees
- White spruce
- Mosses
- Lichens (Lichens are not true plants, but are fungi that live in close association with algae or bacteria.)

Plant adaptations (pages 19, 21, 45):

- Conifer needles and bark ooze sticky resin that smells like turpentine. It protects the trees from plant-eaters because most animals won't even nibble on them.
- Many conifer seeds have "papery" wings that allow them to travel far when the wind blows.
- Conifer needles are covered with a waxy coating that keeps them from drying out.
- Branches of evergreens slant downward so heavy snow slides off.

Types of animals (pages 16–45):

- Squirrels
- Chipmunks
- Spruce grouse
- Red-backed vole
- Deer mice
- Birds: crossbills, gray jays, nutcrackers, nuthatches, warblers, woodpeckers, great gray owls, boreal chickadees
- Foxes
- Snowshoe hares
- Lynx
- Beaver
- Moose
- Black bears
- Elk
- Wolves
- Wolverines

Animal adaptations (pages 23, 28, 31, 35, 39, 41, 42, 44):

- Some animals sleep all through winter in underground burrows or dens (hibernation).
- A crossbill's beak is shaped so that it is easy for them to pry cone scales apart to get to the seeds.
- Gray jays and nutcrackers have strong beaks to tear cones apart to get to the seeds.
- Snowshoe hares' fur changes color so it is hard to see (gray-brown in summer, white in winter).
- Beavers have webbed hind feet and large, flat tails that make them better swimmers.
- Wolverines have large feet and long claws that help make them good climbers.
- Many birds leave the forest at the end of the summer and fly south for the winter to avoid the cold.
- Boreal chickadees tuck seeds into moss and lichens growing on a tree to store them for winter.
- Wolves, foxes, and caribou have thick coats of fur or hair to keep them warm.
- Birds have fluffy feathers to keep them warm.
- Squirrels and nutcrackers hoard seeds all summer to eat during the winter.
- Woodchucks hibernate through the winter until spring.

Name _____   Date _____

Boreal Forests

Boreal Forest Research

Use *A Walk in the Boreal Forests* to fill in the information below. Page numbers have been provided to help you find the information in the book.

Name of ecosystem (or biome): _____

Climate (temperate, polar, or tropical): _____

Climate description (page 10):

_____

_____

Geographic location (pages 6–8):

_____

Types of plants (pages 12–20, 39):

_____

_____

_____

Plant adaptations (pages 19, 21, 45):

_____

_____

_____

_____

_____

Types of animals (pages 16–45):

_____

_____

_____

Animal adaptations (pages 23, 28, 31, 35, 39, 41, 42, 44):

_____

_____

_____

_____

_____

Student Guide

Temperate Deciduous Forests

Read *A Walk in the Deciduous Forest* to learn about the climate in a deciduous forest and the plants and animals that live there.

Lesson Objectives

- Describe two adaptations of plants that live in the temperate deciduous forest (for example, deciduous trees lose their leaves in autumn).
- Identify and describe the characteristics of the temperate deciduous forest (for example, a mild and moist climate with four distinct seasons).
- Describe two adaptations of animals that live in the temperate deciduous forest (for example, frogs have suctions cups on their toes to help them cling to slippery leaves and stems).
- Identify two animals found in the temperate deciduous forest (for example, mice, blue jays, and black bears).
- Identify two plants found in the temperate deciduous forest (for example, ferns, dogwood, and oak trees).

PREPARE

Approximate lesson time is 60 minutes.

Materials

For the Student

> Reading Guide
> Deciduous Forest Research
> *A Walk in the Deciduous Forest* by Rebecca L Johnson

Keywords and Pronunciation

biome (BIY-ohm): A large area with a distinctive community of animals and plants that live in an area with a similar climate. The tundra is a biome that covers a large area of the northern part of all the continents in the northern hemisphere.

deciduous (dih-SIH-juh-wuhs)

stomata (STOH-muh-tuh): Tiny openings in a leaf that allow gases to pass in and out. When the water in leaves evaporates, it escapes through the stomata.

LEARN

Activity 1: A Walk in the Deciduous Forest *(Online)*

Instructions

Use the book to complete the Deciduous Forest Research activity sheet.

Safety

As usual, you will want to preview any websites or recommended reading materials before having your student view them.

Activity 2: Deciduous Forest Research *(Offline)*

Use the book to complete the Deciduous Forest Research activity sheet.

ASSESS

Lesson Assessment: Temperate Deciduous Forests *(Offline)*

Sit with an adult to review the assessment questions.

LEARN

Activity 3: Leaf Observations *(Offline)*

Leaves Can Identify Types of Trees

Leaves have many shapes and sizes, and it is important to observe leaves when you are trying to identify trees. Use the Web links to see examples of different types of leaves. Concentrate on leaf type, shape, and edge. You can describe many different types of leaves using just a few terms. Once you have become familiar with the shapes of leaves, see if you can use your knowledge to identify some trees.

Leaf type	Leaf edges
Simple - having one leaf	Smooth
Compound - having two or more leaflets	Lobed
Needles (conifers)	Wavy (sinuate)
Scales (conifers)	Toothed (serrated)
Leaf arrangement	**Leaf shape**
Opposite - leaves or leaflets directly across from each other on a twig	Pinnate - leaf or leaflet with a strong central vein, or midrib
Alternate - leaves or leaflets staggered down a twig	Palmate - leaf that fans out from a common point, like your thumb and fingers on your hand
Whorled - two or three leaves that form a circular pattern	

Observe the veins that carry nutrients and water to and from the leaves. You may wish to use a magnifier. By making leaf rubbings, keep a record of the leaf types you collected.

1. Place piece of scrap paper under the leaf so the chlorophyll (green pigment) does not stain the work surface when you make your rubbing.

2. Carefully flatten the leaf and place the plain white paper on top.

3. Use the side of a crayon to rub over the leaf to show its texture and shape. Make sure you rub the entire leaf.

4. Label different leaf characteristics, such as simple, compound, lobed, smooth, and palmate.

Name _____   Date _____

Temperate Deciduous Forests
Reading Guide

Using the Reading Guide

Read *A Walk in the Deciduous Forest* by Rebecca L. Johnson. The Words To Know section at the beginning of the book is a glossary with definitions and pronunciations of words in the book. You may find it useful to review these words before you begin reading.

On page 8 of the book is a map of North America, color-coded to show the different ecosystems (or biomes). Begin by having your student point to the region that is the focus of the lesson.

Introduction to Research

Your student will learn about research and note taking by completing a list and answering some questions about each ecosystem. Encourage your student to search the reading for accurate responses and write them in the correct spaces on the list.

Remind your student that taking notes is different from most other types of writing. Notes don't necessarily have to be in complete sentences. Sometimes a simple list is the best way to organize information.

Use the sample list provided to guide your student's reading and note taking. When completing the list, it is not necessary for your student to list all possible answers.

Name of ecosystem (or biome):

- Deciduous forest

Climate (temperate, polar, or tropical):

- Temperate

Climate description (page 10):

- Moist, mild, with four distinct seasons

Geographic locations (pages 6–8):

- Most of the eastern United States
- Also found in Europe and Asia

Types of plants (pages 11–19):

- Maple
- Flowers and wildflowers
- Oak
- Hickory
- Birch
- Ferns
- Hawthorn
- Dogwood
- Virginia creeper
- Wild grape
- Mosses
- Poison ivy

Plant adaptations (pages 15, 38, 39):

- During the winter, tiny new leaves stay safe inside buds.
- Deciduous trees lose their leaves in the autumn and seeds fall with the leaves.

Types of animals (pages 20–45):

- Birds: warblers, vireos, flycatchers, blue jays, woodpeckers, nuthatches, chickadees, hawks, great horned owls
- Mice
- Voles
- Squirrels
- Chipmunks
- Weasels
- Snakes
- Minks
- Cottontail rabbits
- Frogs
- Salamanders
- Raccoons
- Bobcats
- Deer
- Fox
- Black bears
- Caribou

Animal adaptations (pages 26, 28, 35, 40, 42, 43, 44):

- Weasels and minks have slim, flexible bodies that make it easy for them to slip into small spaces in search of food.
- The cottontail rabbit's brownish-gray fur makes it hard to see on the forest floor.
- Frogs have suction cups on their toes to help them cling to slippery leaves and stems.
- The black bear has sharp claws it uses to dig and to climb trees in search of food.
- In the time leading up to winter woodchucks, dormice, raccoons, and bears eat a lot of food; they then live off the fat during the winter.
- Snakes hibernate in an underground burrow during the winter.
- Most birds fly south for the winter, but chickadees, nuthatches, and woodpeckers eat seeds, tree buds, and berries that they have stored.
- Raccoons, bears, and squirrels spend most of the winter days sleeping. The squirrels snack on stored nuts.
- Foxes, bobcats, and weasels have thick coats to keep them warm.

Name _____   Date _____

Temperate Deciduous Forests

Deciduous Forest Research

Use *A Walk in the Deciduous Forest* to fill in the information. Page numbers have been provided to help you find the information in the book.

Name of ecosystem (or biome): _____

Climate (temperate, polar, or tropical): _____

Climate description (page 10):

_____

_____

Geographic location (pages 6–8): _____

Types of plants (pages 11–19):

_____

_____

_____

Plant adaptations (pages 15, 38, 39):

_____

_____

_____

_____

Types of animals (pages 20–45):

_____

_____

_____

Animal adaptations (pages 26, 28, 35, 40, 42, 43, 44):

_____

_____

_____

_____

_____

Student Guide
Tropical Rain Forests

Read *A Walk in the Tropical Rain Forest* to learn about the climate of rain forests and the plants and animals that live there.

Lesson Objectives

- Describe two adaptations of plants that live in the tropical rain forest (for example, plants that live on the forest floor have large leaves to catch plenty of sunlight).
- Identify and describe key characteristics of the tropical rain forest (for example, a warm, wet climate with a constant air temperature and rain every day).
- Describe two adaptations of animals that live in the tropical rain forest (for example, macaws have two toes in the front and two toes in the back so they can grip tree branches like a clamp).
- Identify two animals of the tropical rain forest (for example, spider monkeys, snakes, and macaws).
- Identify two plants of the tropical rain forest (for example, cacao trees and banana plants).

PREPARE

Approximate lesson time is 60 minutes.

Materials

For the Student

Reading Guide
Rain Forest Research
A Walk in the Tropical Rain Forest by Rebecca L. Johnson

Keywords and Pronunciation

biome (BIY-ohm): A large area with a distinctive community of animals and plants and a particular climate. The tundra is a biome that covers a large area of the northern part of the continents in the northern hemisphere.

LEARN

Activity 1: A Walk in the Rain Forest *(Online)*

Safety

As usual, you will want to preview any websites or recommended reading materials listed here.

Activity 2: Rain Forest Research *(Offline)*

Use the book to complete the Rain Forest Research activity sheet.

ASSESS

Lesson Assessment: Tropical Rain Forests *(Offline)*

Sit with an adult to review the assessment questions.

LEARN

Activity 3: Shapely Leaves *(Offline)*

It's All in the Shape of the Leaf

In the tropical rain forest, leaves are wet almost all the time. A layer of water on a leaf can act like a magnifying lens, focusing sunlight and causing the leaf to become too hot. In order to shed water quickly, the leaves of many tropical plants have a waxy coating and a "drip tip" to help carry the water away. In addition, leaf shapes have also adapted to maximize air flow around them, and the increased air flow helps water evaporate so the leaves can dry quickly.

Investigate how leaves with different shapes cope with a very wet climate.

Investigate

1. Cut leaves from aluminum foil in the following shapes:
   - circular and flat
   - long and narrow
   - lobed (deeply curved and rounded edges, such as on an oak or maple)
   - oval with a pointed drip tip and central vein, or mid-rib. To form the leaf's central vein, make a ridge in the foil extending from the leaf stalk (petiole) to the drip tip.
   - one of your own design

2. Tape the leaves to a stick and hold them horizontally over a sink or large bowl.

3. Mist them with a spray bottle.

Conclude

Which leaf shape works best to shed water?

Activity 4: Plant Needs *(Online)*

Name _____   Date _____

Tropical Rain Forests
Reading Guide

Using the Reading Guide

Read *A Walk in the Rain Forest* by Rebecca L. Johnson. The Words To Know section at the beginning of the book is a glossary with definitions and pronunciations of words in the book. You may find it useful to review these words before you begin reading.

On page 8 of the book there is a map of North America, color-coded to show the different ecosystems (or biomes). Begin by having your student point to the region that is the focus of the lesson.

Introduction to Research

Your student will learn about research and note taking by completing a list and answering some questions about each ecosystem. Encourage your student to search the reading for accurate responses and write them in the correct spaces on the list.

Remind your student that taking notes is different from most other types of writing. Notes don't necessarily have to be in complete sentences. Sometimes a simple list is the best way to organize information.

Use the sample list provided to guide your student's reading and note taking. When completing the list, it is not necessary for your student to list all possible answers.

Name of ecosystem (or biome):

- Rain forest

Climate (temperate, polar, or tropical):

- Tropical

Climate description (page 10):

- Warm and wet, rain almost every day

Geographic location (pages 7–9):

- Near the equator in North America, South America, Africa, and Asia
- From Mexico to Panama

Types of plants (pages 10–31):

- Flowers: orchids, bromeliads
- Vines: lianas, strangler fig
- Banana plant
- Small trees and bushes
- Cashew trees
- Cacao tree
- Cannonball tree

Plant adaptations (pages 16, 26, 28, 29):

- Plants on the forest floor have large leaves to catch plenty of sunlight.
- The long, spiky leaves of the bromeliad form a cup that catches water.
- Many leaves are thick and waxy with pointed "drip tips" that shed water quickly.

Types of animals (pages 10–45):

- Birds: hummingbirds, macaws, bellbirds, manakins
- Poison dart frogs
- Crocodiles
- Monkeys: squirrel monkey, black howlers, capuchins, spider monkeys
- Sloths
- Iguana
- Tamandua
- Land crabs
- Snakes
- White-lipped peccaries
- Jaguars

Animal adaptations (pages 20, 22, 23, 24, 32, 33, 37):

- Hummingbirds have long, slender bills that let them reach the nectar inside flowers.
- Macaw feet have two toes in front and two toes in back so they can grip tree branches like a clamp.
- Capuchin monkeys have a prehensile tail that they wrap around trees to help them hold on.
- Sloths have sharp claws that help them hang upside down from trees.
- The fur on the sloth grows from its belly to its back, allowing rainwater to run off as it hangs upside down.
- An iguana's long toes and sharp claws help it scramble up and down trees.
- Tree frogs use their round, sticky toes to cling to slippery stems.
- Their large eyes help tree frogs see well in the dim light of the understory.
- The tamandua uses its long claws and prehensile tail to climb trees looking for ants.

Name _____   Date _____

Tropical Rain Forests

Tropical Rain Forest Research

Use *A Walk in the Rain Forest* to fill in the information. Page numbers have been provided to help you find the information in the book.

Name of ecosystem (or biome): _____

Climate (temperate, polar, or tropical): _____

Climate description (page 10):

_____

_____

Geographic location (pages 7–9): _____

Types of plants (pages 10–31):

_____

_____

_____

Plant adaptations (pages 16, 26, 28, 29):

_____

_____

_____

_____

_____

Types of animals (pages 10–45):

_____

_____

_____

Animal adaptations (pages 20, 22, 23, 24, 32, 33, 37):

_____

_____

_____

_____

_____

Student Guide

Deserts

What makes a desert different from a tropical rain forest? Read *A Walk in the Desert* to learn about the climate, plants, and animals that live in the desert.

Lesson Objectives

- Describe two adaptations of animals in the desert (for example, being active at night to avoid the daytime heat, and long ears that help keep some animals cool).
- Describe two adaptations that help plants survive in the desert (for example, shallow roots that take in water quickly, and a waxy outer coating that helps some plants retain water).
- Identify and describe key characteristics of the desert (for example, extreme temperatures, rainfall of less than 25 cm per year, and the presence of sand dunes).
- Identify two animals that live in the desert (for example, snake, desert tortoise, and cactus wren).
- Identify two plants that live in the desert (for example, barrel cactus, owl clover, and snapdragon).

PREPARE

Approximate lesson time is 60 minutes.

Materials

For the Student

Desert Research
A Walk in the Desert by Rebecca L. Johnson

Keywords and Pronunciation

biome (BIY-ohm)**:** A large area with a distinctive community of animals and plants and a particular climate. The tundra is a biome that covers a large area of the northern part of the continents in the northern hemisphere.

nocturnal (nahk-TUHR-nl)**:** An animal that is active at night. When the sun sets, nocturnal animals become active.

LEARN

Activity 1: A Walk in the Desert *(Online)*

Read *A Walk in the Desert* by Rebecca L. Johnson. The Words to Know section at the beginning of the book is a glossary with definitions and pronunciations of words in the book. You may find it useful to review these words before you begin reading.

Use the book to complete the Desert Research activity sheet.

Safety

As usual, you will want to preview any websites or recommended reading materials listed here.

Activity 2: Desert Research *(Offline)*

ASSESS

Lesson Assessment: Deserts (Offline)

Sit with an adult to review the assessment questions.

LEARN

Activity 3: Optional: A Waxy Coating (Offline)

The waxy coating on the stems of cactus plants helps cactus survive the dry desert climate. The coating helps keep water inside the stem so the plant has access to water, even when there is very little rain.

But can a thin coat of wax really help a plant hold onto water in a dry place like a desert?

Investigate

1. Make two stacks of six paper towels each.

2. Roll each stack tightly into a column.

3. Secure each column at the ends and in the middle with rubber bands.

4. Soak both paper-towel columns in water. Be sure that the paper towels are completely wet, but not dripping excessively.

5. Roll wax paper around one column and secure it with rubber bands at the ends and in the middle.

6. Put both paper-towel columns on the cookie sheet in a warm, sunny spot. Wait 90 minutes. Remove the paper-towel columns from the cookie sheet and unroll them.

Conclude

What do you notice about the paper towels? Which one is wetter? [1] Why do you think this is so? [2] Would water probably stay longer in a stem *with* a waxy coating or a stem *without* a waxy coating? How would the waxy coating help a plant in the desert?

Safety

The metal cookie sheet may become extremely hot. Use oven mitts to handle the cookie sheet and any metal objects left in the sun for a long time.

Name _____   Date _____

Deserts

Desert Research

Use *A Walk in the Desert* to fill in the information and answer the questions below. Page numbers have been provided to help you find the information in the book.

Name of ecosystem (or biome): _____

Climate (temperate, polar, or tropical): _____

Climate description (page 11, 12, 18, 33):

_____

_____

Geographic location (page 6): _____

Types of plants (pages 14, 15, 16, 17, 19, 21, 24, 35, 44):

_____

_____

_____

Plant adaptations (pages 9, 14, 18, 19):

_____

_____

_____

_____

_____

Types of animals (pages 5, 22-32, 34-35, 38-41, 43):

_____

_____

_____

Animal adaptations (pages 28, 29, 32-34, 44):

_____

_____

_____

_____

_____

1. Describe two adaptations that help plants survive in the desert.

_____

_____

_____

_____

2. Describe two adaptations that help animals survive in the desert.

_____

_____

_____

_____

Student Guide

Grasslands

What do grasslands and prairies have in common? Prairies are one type of grassland. Read *A Walk in the Prairie* to learn about the climate and the plants and animals that live in the grasslands.

Lesson Objectives

- Describe an adaptation that helps animals survive in the prairie (for example, birds build nests on the ground because there are few trees, and small animals hibernate through the cold winter months).
- Describe an adaptation that helps plants survive in the prairie (for example, strong roots that spread wide and reach deep into the soil to anchor the plant against winds).
- Identify and describe key characteristics of the prairie (for example, hot summers and cold winters, average rainfall of 25-50 cm per year, and frequent wildfires).
- Identify two animals that live in the prairie (for example, crickets, coyotes, and blackbirds).
- Identify two plants that live in the prairie (for example, wild roses, cattails, and wild clover).

PREPARE

Approximate lesson time is 60 minutes.

Materials

For the Student

Prairie Research
A Walk in the Prairie by Rebecca L. Johnson

Keywords and Pronunciation

biome (BIY-ohm): A large area with a distinctive community of animals and plants and a particular climate. The tundra is a biome that covers a large area of the northern part of the continents in the northern hemisphere.

prairie: A region of cool, temperate grassland that is too dry for trees to grow in. A prairie is one type of grassland. The savanna is another.

LEARN

Activity 1: A Walk in the Prairie *(Online)*

Safety

As usual, you may wish to preview any books or websites listed in this lesson.

Activity 2: Prairie Research *(Online)*

ASSESS

Lesson Assessment: Grasslands *(Offline)*

Sit with an adult to review the assessment questions.

Name _____   Date _____

Grasslands

Prairie Research

Use *A Walk in the Prairie* to fill in the information and answer the questions below. Page numbers have been provided to help you find the information in the book.

Name of ecosystem (or biome): _____

Climate (temperate, polar, or tropical): _____

Climate description (page 10, 11, 16, 18, 42-45):

_____

_____

Geographic location (pages 7, 8): _____

Types of plants (pages 10, 14-15, 17, 22-24):

_____

_____

_____

Plant adaptations (pages 16-18):

_____

_____

_____

_____

_____

Types of animals (pages 5, 26-43):

_____

_____

_____

Animal adaptations (pages 40, 43, 45):

_____

_____

_____

_____

1. Describe two adaptations that help plants survive in the prairie.

_____

_____

_____

2. Describe two adaptations that help animals survive in the prairie.

_____

_____

_____

Student Guide
Freshwater Ecosystems

Freshwater ecosystems are found in almost every part of the world. Ponds are one type of freshwater ecosystem. See how certain plants and animals have become "pond specialists," and learn about a scientist who became a pond specialist, too!

Lesson Objectives

- Describe some adaptations of animals in a pond (for example, the long legs and lightweight body of the water strider, which allow the insect to walk on the surface of the water).
- Describe some adaptations that help plants survive in a pond (for example, the smooth, waxy leaves of the pond lily, which float on top of the water).
- Describe two main characteristics of a pond (for example, fresh water, calm water, shallow enough for sunlight to reach the bottom).
- Identify two animals you might find in a pond (for example, frogs and dragonflies).
- Identify two plants you might find in the pond (for example, water lilies and cattails).
- State that Ann Morgan was a scientist who studied pond life.

PREPARE

Approximate lesson time is 60 minutes.

Materials

For the Student

Pond Research

Keywords and Pronunciation

freshwater: Water that contains very little salt.

LEARN

Activity 1: Freshwater Ponds *(Online)*

Select the forward arrow to visit a freshwater pond

Safety

As usual, you may wish to preview any books or websites listed in this lesson.

Activity 2: Pond Research *(Online)*

ASSESS

Lesson Assessment: Freshwater Ecosystems *(Offline)*

Sit with an adult to review the assessment questions.

LEARN

Activity 3: A Pond Visit *(Offline)*

Safety

Supervise children at all times when visiting a pond, and use extreme caution when working near the edge of a pond or any other body of water.

Name _____   Date _____

Freshwater Ecosystems

Pond Research

Use the Explore section to fill in the information and answer the question below.

Name of ecosystem (or biome): _____

Climate (temperate, polar, or tropical): _____

Geographic location: _____

Types of plants:

_____

_____

Plant adaptations:

_____

_____

_____

_____

Types of animals:

_____

_____

_____

Animal adaptations:

_____

_____

_____

_____

1. How did Ann Morgan learn about aquatic life?

_____

_____

_____

Student Guide

Marine Ecosystems

Like freshwater ecosystems, marine ecosystems exist in almost every part of the world. Coral reefs are one type of marine ecosystem. Explore a coral reef to learn about the plants and animals that live there.

Lesson Objectives

- Describe an adaptation of a plant that lives in the coral reef (for example, zooxanthelle lives with corals to get the carbon dioxide it needs to grow).
- Describe an adaptation of an animal that lives in the coral reef (for example, the wavy arms of corals are designed to catch food).
- Identify a plant that lives in the coral reef (for example, phytoplankton, zooxanthelle).
- Identify a type of animal that lives in the coral reef (for example, sponges, corals, sharks, parrotfish).
- Identify and describe key characteristics of the coral reef (for example, warm, tropical water; wave action; plenty of sunlight).

PREPARE

Approximate lesson time is 60 minutes.

Advance Preparation

- In the optional activity, Strong Sea Star, your student will demonstrate how a sea star can open a mussel shell. If you choose to do the activity, you will need to purchase four sturdy suction cups of uniform size, at least 5 centimeters in diameter. You can buy them at most craft or hardware stores.

Materials

For the Student

Coral Reef Research

Keywords and Pronunciation

atoll (A-tahl)

biome (BIY-ohm) : A large area with a distinctive community of animals and plants and a particular climate. The tundra is a biome that covers a large area of the northern part of the continents in the northern hemisphere.

ecosystem (EE-koh-sis-tuhm) : A community or group of organisms living and interacting with each other and their environment.

marine: Anything having to do with the sea and the living and nonliving things in the sea. The plants and animals in a marine environment need saltwater to survive.

phytoplankton (fiy-toh-PLANGK-tuhn)

zooxanthelle (zoh-uh-zan-THEH-luh)

LEARN

Activity 1: The Coral Reef: A Marine Ecosystem *(Online)*

Activity 2: Coral Reef Research *(Online)*

Continue to research the different ecosystems of the world as you learn about the coral reef.

ASSESS

Lesson Assessment: Marine Ecosystems *(Offline)*

Sit with an adult to review the assessment questions.

LEARN

Activity 3: Strong Sea Star *(Offline)*

Instructions

Investigate

1. Generously moisten a paper towel and place it on a table or countertop.
2. Press one suction cup onto the wet paper towel, then press it firmly onto the refrigerator door, near the handle.
3. Try to open the door by pulling on the hook attached to the suction cup. Were you able to open the door?
4. Moisten a second suction cup and press it on the refrigerator next to the first suction cup.
5. Pull on both suction cups to try and open the door. Were you able to open the door using two suction cups?
6. Repeat the procedure adding the third and then the fourth suction cup. You will need a helper to pull on two of the four suction cups.

Conclude

Was it easier to open the door with one suction cup or four?

A sea star doesn't have hands, so how does it open the shells of animals that it wants to eat?

The arms of a sea star have suction-cup adaptations. A sea star can attach its arms to many things, such as mussels, and pull them open, just as you did the refrigerator door!

Name _____   Date _____

Marine Ecosystems

Coral Reef Research

Use the Explore section to fill in the information and answer the questions below.

Name of ecosystem (or biome): _____

Climate (temperate, polar, or tropical): _____

Climate description:

_____

_____

Geographic location : _____

Types of plants:

_____

_____

_____

Plant adaptations:

_____

_____

_____

_____

_____

Types of animals:

_____

_____

_____

Animal adaptations:

_____

_____

_____

_____

_____

1. Use your notes to describe one adaptation that helps plants survive in the coral reef.

_____

_____

_____

2. Use your notes to describe one adaptation that helps animals survive in the coral reef.

_____

_____

_____

Student Guide
Changes in Ecosystems

There are a lot of different factors (things) that make up an ecosystem. Changes in temperature, sunlight, and rainfall can change an ecosystem. Learn about the different ways plants and animals change and adapt when an ecosystem changes. Research a problem caused by changes in an ecosystem and make a claim based on merit to fix the problem.

Lesson Objectives

- Explain changes that can happen in an ecosystem and how that affects plant and animal life.
- Conduct research on a specific problem caused by changes in an ecosystem.
- Identify solutions to address and correct changes in an ecosystem that disrupt plant and animal life.
- Analyze and make a claim about the merit of a solution to a problem caused when the environment changes and has an impact on plants and animals.

PREPARE

Approximate lesson time is 60 minutes.

Keywords and Pronunciation

carbon dioxide: A gas that, in large quantities, leads to global warming

fossil fuels: Coal, oil, and natural gas that come from old organic matter

invasive species: A species introduced and thriving in an ecosystem not of its origin that disrupts the ecosystem

merit-based solution: A solution that has lots of supportive evidence

pesticide: Chemicals used to protect crops from insects and other pests

LEARN

Activity 1: Types Changes in Ecosystems *(Online)*

Activity 2: Ecosystem Solutions *(Online)*

Research a specific problem facing an ecosystem. Use the examples provided to make a merit-based claim to address the ecosystem problem.

Activity 3: Lesson Review *(Online)*

ASSESS

Lesson Assessment: Changes in Ecosystems *(Online)*

You will complete an online assessment covering the main objectives of the lesson.

Student Guide
Adapting to Change

Plants and animals that adapt to change are more likely to succeed and survive. Learn about different plants and animals that have been able to adapt and pass along positive traits to their offspring.

Lesson Objectives

- Explain and provide supporting evidence showing how the variations in characteristics among individuals of the same species may provide advantages in surviving, finding mates, or reproducing.
- Analyze or interpret data to provide evidence that plants and animals have traits inherited from parents and that variation of these traits exists in a group of similar organisms.

PREPARE

Approximate lesson time is 60 minutes.

Materials

For the Student

Family Traits Assignment

Keywords and Pronunciation

adapt: make changes that help an animal succeed or survive

LEARN

Activity 1: Traits and Survival *(Online)*

Activity 2: Family Traits *(Online)*

Activity 3: Best Traits for Survival *(Online)*

Safety

Preview any recommended websites before having your student view them.

Activity 4: Trait Advantages *(Online)*

Activity 5: Lesson Review *(Online)*

ASSESS

Lesson Assessment: Adapting to Change *(Offline)*

Sit with an adult to review the assessment questions.

Name _____   Date _____

Assignment

Family Traits

Investigate the eight family traits in the chart below and interview family members to determine whether or not they have these traits. Record your results in the table.

Trait	Results
1. earlobe attachment (record Y for yes and N for no)	
2. color blindness (record Y for yes and N for no)	
3. curly or straight hair (record C for curly and S for straight)	
4. tongue rolling (record Y for yes and N for no)	
5. dimples (record Y for yes and N for no)	
6. right/left handed (record R for right and L for left)	
7. freckles (record Y for yes and N for no)	
8. hand clasping (record R for right and L for left)	

1. Look over the data you collected. Do all of your family members have the same traits?

   _____

   _____

   _____

   _____

2. Why do people from the same family sometimes have different traits?

_____

_____

_____

_____

3. Think about the traits listed. Which traits listed give an advantage?

_____

_____

_____

_____

Student Guide
Ecosystems: Unit Review and Assessment

Congratulations! You've visited ecosystems all over the world, from tundra to desert to coral reefs. Show how much you've learned about the world's climate zones and the ecosystems within them.

Lesson Objectives

- Recognize that living things have both physical and behavioral adaptations that enable them to survive in a particular ecosystem.
- Define *climate* as the usual weather in a certain area over many years.
- Demonstrate mastery of the knowledge and skills taught in this unit.
- Describe different ecosystems (tundra, boreal forest, deciduous forest, tropical rain forest, grasslands, desert, freshwater, and marine).
- Explain that an *ecosystem* includes all living and nonliving things interacting in a particular region.
- Identify the three main climate zones as tropical, temperate, and polar.
- Recognize that scientists use patterns of climate, vegetation, and animal life to identify different ecosystems.
- Explain that an *ecosystem* includes all living and nonliving things that interact in a particular region.
- Define *climate* as the usual weather pattern in a certain area over many years.
- Describe an adaptation of an animal that lives in the coral reef (for example, the wavy arms of corals are designed to catch food).
- Describe an adaptation that helps animals survive in the prairie (for example, birds build nests on the ground because there are few trees, and small animals hibernate through the cold winter months).
- Describe some adaptations of animals in a pond (for example, the long legs and lightweight body of the water strider, which allow the insect to walk on the surface of the water).
- Describe some adaptations that help plants survive in a pond (for example, the smooth, waxy leaves of the pond lily, which float on top of the water).
- Describe two adaptations of animals in the desert (for example, being active at night to avoid the daytime heat, and long ears that help keep some animals cool).
- Describe two adaptations of plants that live in the tropical rain forest (for example, plants that live on the forest floor have large leaves to catch plenty of sunlight).
- Identify and describe key characteristics of the desert (for example, extreme temperatures, rainfall of less than 25 cm per year, and the presence of sand dunes).
- Identify and describe key characteristics of the tropical rain forest (for example, a warm, wet climate with a constant air temperature and rain every day).
- Identify and describe key characteristics of the tundra (for example, a cold, dry, and harsh climate).
- Identify and describe the characteristics of the temperate deciduous forest (for example, a mild and moist climate with four distinct seasons).

PREPARE

Approximate lesson time is 60 minutes.

Keywords and Pronunciation

boreal (BOR-ee-uhl)

deciduous (dih-SIH-juh-wuhs)

tundra (TUN-druh)

LEARN

Activity 1: Ecosystems *(Online)*

ASSESS

Unit Assessment: Ecosystems *(Offline)*

Complete an offline Unit Assessment. Your learning coach will score the assessment.

Student Guide

Optional: Animals of the Ancient Reefs

What lives in the ocean's coral reefs? Have coral reefs changed over time? See how scientists view ancient reefs to compare the plants and animals of today with those from the ancient Silurian period.

Lesson Objectives

- Recognize that scientists think that many kinds of animals that once lived in coral reefs have completely disappeared.
- Recognize that scientists think that some animals alive today in reefs resemble animals of the past.

PREPARE

Approximate lesson time is 60 minutes.

Keywords and Pronunciation

Cenozoic (see-nuh-ZOH-ihk)

cephalopod (SEH-fuh-luh-pahd)

crinoid (KRIY-noyd)

evidence: A thing or information used to form a conclusion or make a judgment. Evidence leads scientists to think that coral reefs similar to the reefs of today existed in the distant past.

extinct: No longer existing. A group of living things that has died out. Scientists have evidence that trilobytes became extinct a long time ago.

Mesozoic (meh-zuh-ZOH-ihk)

Paleozoic (pay-lee-uh-ZOH-ihk)

receptaculid (ree-sep-TAK-kyuh-lihd)

Silurian (sih-LOUR-ee-uhn)

Silurian period: A period of time used by scientists to discuss the ancient past that began 438 million years ago and lasted about 40 million years. Scientists think coral reefs thrived in warm, shallow waters during the Silurian period.

stromatoporoid (stroh-muh-tuh-POR-oyd)

trilobite (TRIY-luh-biyt)

LEARN

Activity 1: Optional: Lesson Instructions (*Online*)

This lesson is OPTIONAL. It is provided for students who seek enrichment or extra practice. You may skip this lesson.

If you choose to skip this lesson, then go to the Plan or Lesson Lists page and mark this lesson "Skipped" in order to proceed to the next lesson in the course.

Activity 2: Optional: The Ancient Reef (*Online*)

Activity 3: Optional: Changes in the Reef (*Online*)

Which animals that scientists think lived in reefs long ago are similar to ones living in reefs today? Which animals are now extinct?

List your answers in your Science Notebook. Before you begin, think about how you can set up your page to sort animals into two groups.

Activity 4: Optional: A Virtual Tour from Past to Present (*Online*)

Student Guide

Optional: Plants and Animals of the Ancient Forests

What do scientists think lived in the forests of long ago? Journey through an ancient forest to learn more about the plants and animals that lived there.

Lesson Objectives

- Explain that when the environment changes, some plants and animals survive and reproduce, while others either die off or move to new locations.
- Classify dinosaurs as either herbivores (plant eaters) or carnivores (meat eaters).

PREPARE

Approximate lesson time is 60 minutes.

Materials

For the Student

> Dinosaur Sort

Keywords and Pronunciation

apatosaurus (uh-pa-tuh-SAWR-us)

carnivore (KAHR-nuh-vor)**:** An animal that feeds mainly on other animals. A tiger is considered a carnivore since its diet is mainly other animals.

cycad (SIY-kuhd)

cycads: A group of evergreen plants that have cones. I could tell which trees were cycads by the cones on their branches.

extinct: No longer existing. A group of living things that has died out. Scientists have evidence that trilobytes became extinct a long time ago.

herbivore (UR-buh-vor)**:** An animal that feeds mainly on plants. A cow is considered an herbivore since its diet is mainly plants.

herrarasaurus (huh-rair-uh-SAWR-us)

icarosaurus (ih-kuh-ruh-SAWR-uhs)

melanosaurus (muh-lan-uh-SAWR-uhs)

mussaurus (mous-SAWR-uhs)

plateosaurus (play-tee-uh-SAWR-uhs)

staurikosaurus (staw-rih-kuh-SAWR-uhs)

stegosaurus (steh-guh-SAWR-uhs)

Triassic period: A period that began 245 million years ago. Scientists think dinosaurs lived during the Triassic period.

triceratops (triy-SEHR-uh-tahps)

LEARN

Activity 1: Optional: Lesson Instructions (*Online*)

Activity 2: Optional: The Ancient Forests (*Online*)

Activity 3: Optional: Dinosaur Sort (*Offline*)

Instructions

1. Discuss each dinosaur.

2. Sort the dinosaurs.

3. Sort by claws, armor, and height.

4. Sort by diet.

Activity 4: Optional: How Tall Were They? (*Offline*)

Activity 5: Optional: What Dinosaurs Lived in Your Backyard? (*Online*)

Activity 6: Optional: Read a Book (*Offline*)

Name _____   Date _____

Plants and Animals of the Ancient Forests
Dinosaur Sort

Triceratops

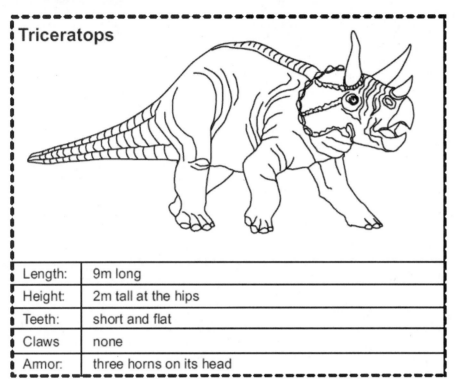

Length:	9m long
Height:	2m tall at the hips
Teeth:	short and flat
Claws	none
Amor:	three horns on its head

Velociraptor

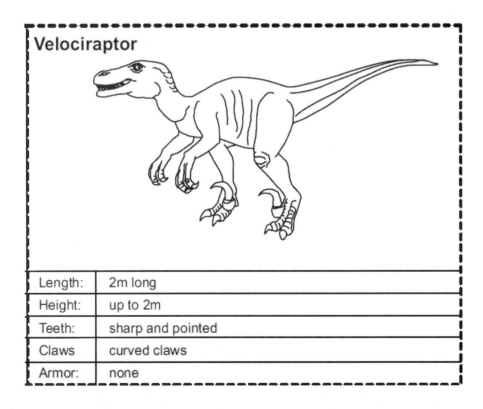

Length:	2m long
Height:	up to 2m
Teeth:	sharp and pointed
Claws	curved claws
Armor:	none

Name _____   Date _____

Allosaurus

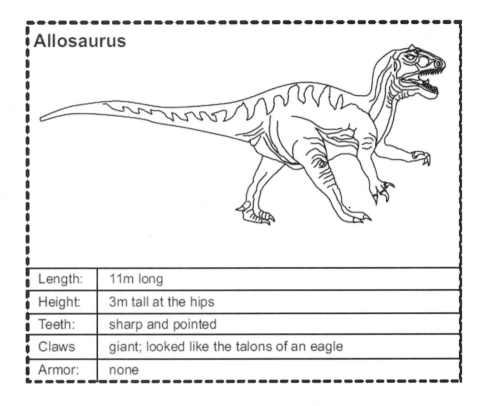

Length:	11m long
Height:	3m tall at the hips
Teeth:	sharp and pointed
Claws	giant; looked like the talons of an eagle
Armor:	none

Stegosaurus

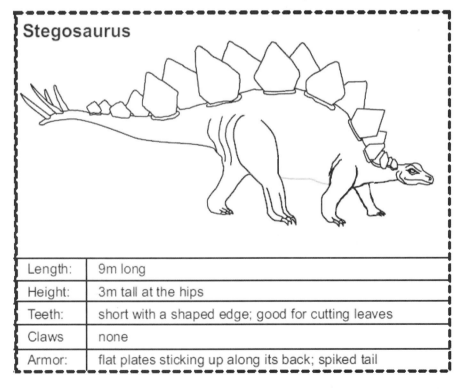

Length:	9m long
Height:	3m tall at the hips
Teeth:	short with a shaped edge; good for cutting leaves
Claws	none
Armor:	flat plates sticking up along its back; spiked tail

Name _____   Date _____

Tyrannosaurus

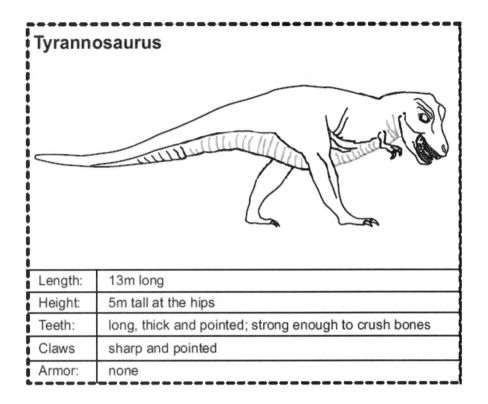

Length:	13m long
Height:	5m tall at the hips
Teeth:	long, thick and pointed; strong enough to crush bones
Claws:	sharp and pointed
Armor:	none

Apatosaurus

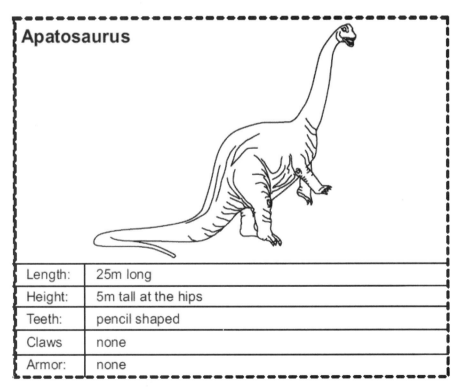

Length:	25m long
Height:	5m tall at the hips
Teeth:	pencil shaped
Claws:	none
Armor:	none

Student Guide

Optional: Animals of the Ancient Tundra

How do scientists think so many large animals survived the cold climate on our planet during the Ice Age? What happened to the woolly mammoth and the sabre-toothed cat? Where are all these big animals today?

Lesson Objectives

- Explain that when the environment changes, some plants and animals survive and reproduce, while others either die off or move to new locations.
- Describe the main characteristics of the woolly mammoth (it is related to the elephant; it ate only plants; it lived in cold, dry grasslands and open tundra).
- Recognize that scientists think that many kinds of animals that once lived on Earth have completely disappeared.
- Recognize that scientists think that some animals alive today resemble animals of the distant past.

PREPARE

Approximate lesson time is 60 minutes.

Keywords and Pronunciation

Cenozoic (see-nuh-ZOH-ihk)

extinct: No longer existing. A group of living things that has died out. Scientists have evidence that trilobytes became extinct a long time ago.

glacier (GLAY-shur): A large mass of ice that forms from snow piling up over many years, and which moves slowly over the surface of the Earth. Glaciers covered a large part of the Earth during the Pleistocene epoch.

ice age: A generally cool period of time on Earth when large areas of the planet are covered with glaciers. Many tundra animals that lived during the Ice Age are now extinct.

Mesozoic (meh-zuh-ZOH-ihk)

Paleozoic (pay-lee-uh-ZOH-ihk)

Pleistocene (PLIYS-tuh-seen)

Pleistocene epoch: A period of time that scientists define as beginning one and a half million years ago and ending only 11,000 years ago—a relatively recent epoch in geologic time. Many kinds of plants and animals that lived during the Pleistocene epoch still exist today.

Silurian (sih-LOUR-ee-uhn)

Triassic (triy-A-sihk)

tundra (TUN-druh)

LEARN

Activity 1: Optional: Lesson Instructions (*Online*)

Activity 2: Optional: The Ancient Tundra (*Online*)

Activity 3: Optional: Changes in the Tundra (*Online*)

Activity 4: Optional: Ice Sampling (*Offline*)

Student Guide

Optional: Methods of Studying Ecosystems of the Past

Scientists have many different methods of learning about the plants, animals, and even climates of long ago. Find out what clues nature provides, from valleys carved by glaciers to the paper-thin rings inside a tree trunk.

Lesson Objectives

- Recognize different types of evidence scientists use to study ecosystems of the past, such as fossils, tree rings, and ice cores.
- Use tree-ring patterns to describe various climate characteristics from the past.

PREPARE

Approximate lesson time is 60 minutes.

Materials

For the Student

  Tree Rings

Keywords and Pronunciation

dendrochronology (dehn-druh-kruh-NAH-luh-jee)**:** The study of tree rings to determine regional patterns of drought and climatic change.

evidence: a thing, or information, used to form a conclusion or make a judgment

LEARN

Activity 1: Optional: Lesson Instructions (*Online*)

Activity 2: Optional: Evidence from Nature's Past *(Online)*

What do cylinders of ancient ice, a chunk of coal, and tree rings have in common? They each tell the story of Earth's past. Matching patterns in nature helps scientists begin to understand our planet's history.

Activity 3: Optional: Tree Rings, Time Keepers of the Past *(Offline)*

Instructions

Tree Ring Basics

Print the Tree Rings pattern sheet. Trace the outermost ring in one color. Trace the ring at the center with another color. Which ring do you think is the oldest, or formed first? [1]

Count the rings on the sample on page 1. This will tell you how old the tree is. [2]

Measure the width of a few rings. What do you think a narrow ring is telling you? Why does a tree grow a narrow ring some years and a wide ring in other years? [3]

Measure the width of a few rings. What do you think a narrow ring is telling you? Why does a tree grow a narrow ring some years and a wide ring in other years? [3]

How Do Patterns Tell Us About the Past?

Print and cut out the 6 sample wedges. Look at each of the samples. Do you see places where the pattern of ring widths looks the same? Some of these trees are older, meaning they lived longer ago in history, than others. See if you can match the ring patterns.

Start with one wedge. Slide each wedge beside it to see if any patterns match. Keep points of the wedges on the same side. When you find a match, leave the wedges in place. Continue until all remaining wedges are joined by matching patterns.

Matching rings formed during the same calendar year. New rings are added on the outside of the wood, just under the bark. If a wide ring that matches on both samples is closer to the bark of one tree, that tree is from an earlier time in history. Check to make sure the patterns line up. Which tree grew longest ago?[4] Which tree grew most recently?[5]

This is how scientists use tree rings to tell us about the past. Each time the pattern of tree rings match, we can reach farther into the past to discover the growing conditions for the oldest tree when it was very young. The science of studying tree rings is called dendrochronology.

Activity 4: Optional: Fossilized by Amber *(Online)*

Name _____   Date _____

Methods of Studying Ecosystems of the Past
Tree Rings

Cut the sample wedge from this tree.

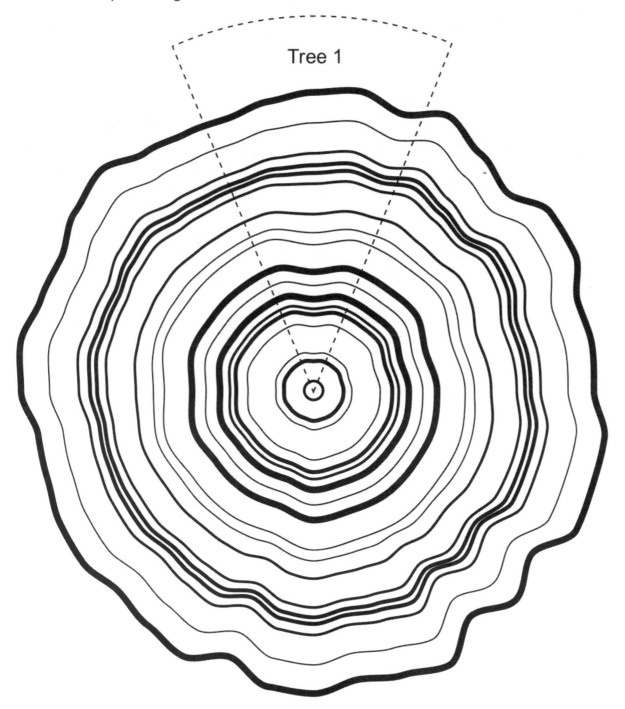

Tree 1

Now cut out these other samples.

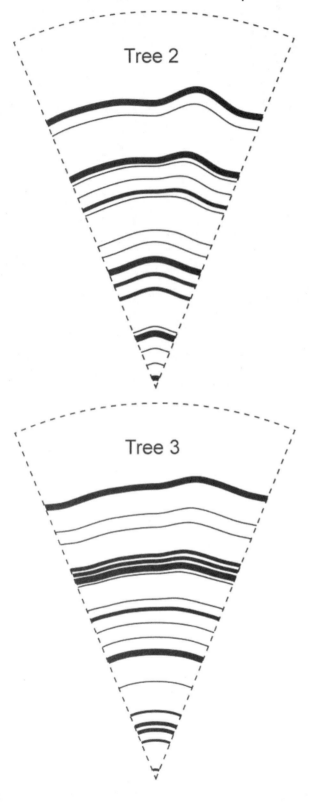

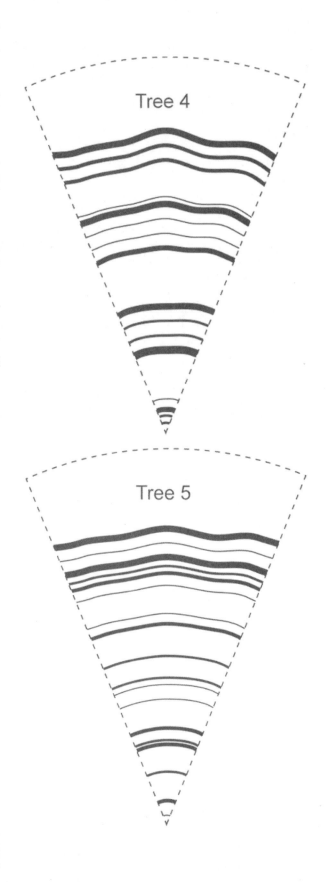

Tree 4

Tree 5

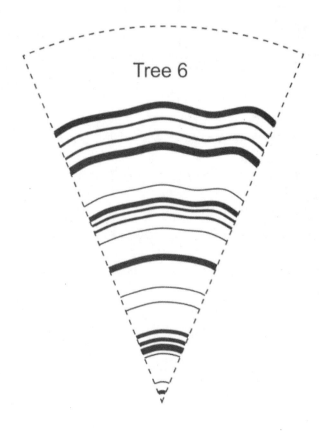

Tree 6

Student Guide

Optional: Ecosystems of the Past: Unit Review

Review what you have learned about the ecosystems of the past and demonstrate your knowledge.

Lesson Objectives

- Explain that when the environment changes, some plants and animals survive and reproduce, while others either die off or move to new locations.
- Compare the climates of modern ecosystems with similar ecosystems from Earth's geologic past, including reef, tundra, and forest.
- Demonstrate mastery of the knowledge and skills taught in this unit.
- Recognize some methods scientists use to study past ecosystems, such as those of examining fossils, tree rings, and ice.
- Recognize that scientists think that many kinds of organisms that once lived on Earth have completely disappeared.
- Recognize that scientists think that some animals and plants alive today resemble those of the past.

PREPARE

Approximate lesson time is 60 minutes.

Materials

For the Student

Ecosystems of the Past Extra Practice

LEARN

Activity 1: Optional: Lesson Instructions (*Online*)

Activity 2: Optional: Ecosystems of the Past Unit Review (*Online*)

Name _____ Date _____

Ecosystems of the Past

Extra Practice

Circle the correct answer.

1. Which methods do scientists use to study ecosystems of the past?

    A. fossils

    B. tree rings

    C. ice

    D. all of the above

2. Which animal do scientists think lived in the ancient tundra but does not live in the tundra today?

    A. woolly mammoth

    B. polar bear

    C. reindeer

    D. musk ox

3. Which statement about the dinosaurs do scientists think is true?

    A. Dinosaurs of the ancient forest were related to the woolly mammoth.

    B. Dinosaurs of the ancient forest have completely disappeared.

    C. Dinosaurs are found in most forests today.

    D. Dinosaurs are found today in the rain forest of Africa.

4. Which relative of today's elephant could be found in the ancient tundra?

    A. bison

    B. trilobite

    C. dinosaur

    D. woolly mammoth

Directions: Answer the following questions in a complete sentence.

5. When the environment changes, some plants and animals are able to survive and reproduce. What can happen to the other animals?

    _____

    _____

    _____

6. Compare and contrast how scientists see the climate of the ancient tundra with the climate of the modern tundra of today.

    _____

    _____

    _____

    _____

    _____

Student Guide

States of Matter

Everything in our natural world is made of matter—the food you eat, the water we drink, even the air we breathe. Understand matter and you can begin to understand nature. Do you know what *really* happens when water boils or an ice pop melts? Experiment with matter and find out!

Lesson Objectives

- Compare the motion of atoms in solids, liquids, and gases (atoms in solids vibrate around a fixed position, atoms in liquids do not stay in a fixed position but remain close to each other, and atoms in gases move freely, bouncing off other atoms but not staying close together most of the time).
- Describe properties of solids, liquids, and gases (for example, solids have a definite shape and a definite volume; liquids have a definite volume but no definite shape; gases have neither a definite shape nor a definite volume).
- Recognize that all matter is made up of particles called *atoms,* which are much too small to see with the naked eye and are constantly in motion.

PREPARE

Approximate lesson time is 60 minutes.

Materials

For the Student

Mystery Substance Lab Sheet

Keywords and Pronunciation

matter: Anything that takes up space and has mass. The three states of matter are solid, liquid, and gas.

properties: Ways of describing an object, such as its size, color, shape, or texture. I listed the properties of the rock as red, rough, and round.

state: Typical forms that matter takes. Solid, liquid, and gas are all states of matter.

LEARN

Activity 1: Matter, Matter, Everywhere *(Online)*

Activity 2: What State of Matter Is It? *(Offline)*

ASSESS

Lesson Assessment: States of Matter *(Offline)*

Sit with an adult to review the assessment questions.

LEARN

Activity 3: Act It Out *(Offline)*

Name _____   Date _____

States of Matter
Mystery Substance Lab Sheet

Predict

Is the mystery matter a gas, a liquid, or a solid? Why do you think so?

_____

_____

Observe

Look at the mystery matter closely. Record your observations below.

Color:

_____

Texture (how does it feel):

_____

Shape:

_____

Smell:

_____

Other observations:

_____

Experiment

Pour the mystery matter into a cup. Then do each test below and record your results on the chart.

Test	What do you observe?	Is this how a liquid acts? Yes or No	Is this how a solid acts? Yes or No
Touch test (fast) Stick your finger through the mystery matter so that it touches the bottom of the cup.			
Shape test Put the mystery matter into another shaped container. Does it stay the same shape or does it fill the new container and take its shape?			
Drip test Pour the mystery matter from one container to another.			
Bounce test Hold the mystery matter 30 cm above the table. Drop it onto the table.			
Ball test Roll the mystery matter into a ball. See if it stays in a ball shape for 10 seconds.			

Test	What do you observe?	Is this how a liquid acts? Yes or No	Is this how a solid acts? Yes or No
Heat test Use the aluminum foil to make a small bowl, about the size of a quarter. Put one teaspoon of the mystery matter in the aluminum foil bowl. Use the clothespin to pick up the bowl. Heat the mystery matter over the lit votive candle.			
Cooling test Set the mystery matter in the aluminum foil bowl aside and let it cool to room temperature.			

Conclude

Look back at your data chart. Is your mystery matter a solid or a liquid? Why?

Was your prediction correct?

_____

_____

_____

_____

_____

Student Guide

Changes in the States of Matter

What do ice, water, and water vapor have in common? Investigate the three states of matter to find out how molecules move as matter changes states.

Lesson Objectives

- Describe how matter changes states by freezing, melting, or boiling when heated.
- State that the *boiling point* is the temperature at which a liquid changes to a gas as it evaporates and a gas changes to a liquid as it condenses.
- State that the melting point and the freezing point is the same temperature at which a solid changes to a liquid and a liquid changes to a solid.

PREPARE

Approximate lesson time is 60 minutes.

Advance Preparation

- Prepare four solutions of water and rubbing alcohol to show how the freezing points of different kinds of matter are not all the same.
- Label four paper cups A, B, C, and D. Use a graduated cylinder to prepare four different solutions of water and alcohol.
- Cup A: 50 mL of water.
- Cup B: 30 mL of water, 20 mL of rubbing alcohol.
- Cup C: 25 mL of water, 25 mL of rubbing alcohol.
- Cup D: 50 mL of rubbing alcohol.
- In an ice cube tray, fill one spot with liquid from Cup A. Repeat with Cups B, C and D. If you need to, make a note of which liquid is in each spot in the tray.
- Put the tray in the freezer until the liquid from Cup A becomes a solid. For best results, leave the tray in the freezer at least 5 hours or overnight.

Materials

For the Student

    Melting Points Lab Sheet
    cup - wide-mouth (4)
    rubbing alcohol - 70%

Keywords and Pronunciation

altitude: The height of a thing above a reference level, especially above sea level or above the Earth's surface. The plane flew at a very high altitude when it passed over the mountains.

condense: To change from gas to liquid. Water vapor condenses on the glass of ice water, forming droplets of liquid water.

evaporate: To change from a liquid into a vapor. Liquids are also said to boil. After the water began to evaporate, it slowly disappeared from the pan.

freeze: The process by which a liquid turns into a solid. Water at the North Pole freezes into glaciers.

melt: The process by which a solid turns into a liquid. You can melt butter in a pan on the stove.

state: Typical forms that matter takes. Solid, liquid, and gas are all states of matter.

LEARN

Activity 1: How Does Matter Change States? *(Online)*

Activity 2: Freezing Points *(Offline)*

Activity 2. Freezing Points (Offline)

Show that the freezing points of different kinds of matter are not all the same, even if most of the matter is water. Mix different amounts of water and isopropyl alcohol, freeze them, and then find their melting points (same as their freezing points).

1. Label four wide-mouth cups A, B, C, and D. Use a measuring cylinder to prepare four different liquids:

   Cup A: 150 mL of water

   Cup B: 90 mL of water, 60 mL of rubbing alcohol

   Cup C: 75 mL of water, 75 mL of rubbing alcohol

   Cup D: 150 mL of rubbing alcohol

3. Put the cups in the freezer until the liquid from Cup A becomes a solid. For best results, leave the cups in the freezer at least 5 hours or overnight.

4. Transfer the ice block formed from Cup A to a resealable sandwich bag. Label the bag "Cup A."

5. Carefully crush the frozen sample in its bag using a rolling pin or other heavy object.

6. Hold the bag at the top so that the heat of your hand does not change the temperature of the sample.

7. Insert the thermometer into the bag every 30 seconds. Record the temperature.

TIP: Once a small pool of water forms, measure the temperature of the water, not the ice chips.

8. Continue recording the temperatures for 4 minutes.

9. Repeat the same procedure with the blocks from Cups B, C, and D.

Conclude

Look at your data. What conclusions can you make about the freezing points of the different liquids?

Safety

Supervise children carefully when working with rubbing alcohol. Avoid contact with eyes.

ASSESS

Lesson Assessment: Changes in the States of Matter (*Online*)

You will complete an online assessment covering the main objectives of the lesson.

Name _____ Date _____

Changes in the States of Matter
Melting Points Lab Sheet

Predict

Do all frozen liquids melt at the same temperature?

_____

_____

Experiment

Cup A 150 mL water	Cup B 90 mL water 60 mL rubbing alcohol	Cup C 75 mL water 75 mL rubbing alcohol	Cup D 150 mL rubbing alcohol
°C			

Conclude

Look at your data. Did all frozen liquids melt at the same temperature?

_____

What conclusion can you draw about the melting points of the different cups?

_____

_____

_____

Student Guide

Length and Volume

How long is an eyelash? How much water will fit in a bathtub? Can you measure eyelashes and water with the same unit of measurement? Measure the lengths and volumes of several objects using various units of measurement.

Lesson Objectives

- Define *volume* as the amount of space occupied by matter, or the amount of space inside a container.
- Use appropriate tools to measure in metric units the length, volume, mass, and weight of different objects.
- Convert measurements from centimeters to millimeters.
- Convert measurements from meters to centimeters.
- Estimate and measure the length of various objects.
- Estimate and measure the volume of various objects.

PREPARE

Approximate lesson time is 60 minutes.

Keywords and Pronunciation

meniscus (muh-NIS-kuhs)**:** A curved upper surface of a column of liquid. When we looked at the cylinder from the side, we could see the water's meniscus.

prefix: One or more syllables that can be attached to the front of another word to change its meaning. In the word millimeter, milli- is a prefix.

volume: The amount of space something takes up, or the amount of space inside a container. We measured the volume of the jar at 2 liters.

LEARN

Activity 1: Measuring Matter *(Online)*

Activity 2: Measure Length *(Offline)*

1. Divide a piece of notebook paper into four columns. Label the columns Object, Centimeters, Millimeters, and Meters.

2. Gather several household objects of varying lengths that would be best measured in centimeters. Items such as a jump rope, a sofa cushion, a piece of uncooked spaghetti, and a pencil are good choices.

3. Use the metric ruler to measure the lengths of the objects using centimeters. Record the name of each object and its measurement on the chart.

4. Measure the same lengths using millimeters. Note the measurements in the column labeled Millimeters.

Did your student see a numerical relationship between the lengths expressed in centimeters and then in millimeters? Now measure a small object, such as a paper clip, in centimeters, then convert the measurements into millimeters. Note each measurement.

5. Choose different objects whose lengths would best be measured in meters.

6. Using a meter stick, record the lengths of the objects. Draw a line below the previous measurements. Note each measurement in the Meters column below the line.

Activity 3: Measure Volume *(Offline)*

ASSESS

Lesson Assessment: Length and Volume *(Offline)*

Sit with an adult to review the assessment questions.

LEARN

Activity 4: More Marvelous Metrics! *(Online)*

Activity 5: Optional: ZlugQuest Measurement *(Online)*

Student Guide
Mass and Weight

Imagine going to the moon as an astronaut. Would you weigh the same there as you do here on Earth? No. On the moon you could bounce all around because you would weigh less. But how is that possible? Your body is the same size and shape. It's made of the same stuff. The answer is that your body's *mass* doesn't change, but its *weight* does. Discover the difference between mass and weight.

Lesson Objectives

- Recognize that *mass* is a measure of the resistance of an object to acceleration by a force.
- Recognize that the mass of an object stays the same, but the object's weight changes depending on where in the universe the object is being weighed.
- Define *kilogram* as a unit of mass, and *milligram* and *gram* as related units.
- Explain that *mass* is the amount of matter in an object, whereas *weight* is the force exerted by gravity on an object.

PREPARE

Approximate lesson time is 60 minutes.

Advance Preparation

- In this Science lesson, your student will begin to understand mass by observing the force needed to move large and small blocks of ice. Prepare the ice blocks at least one day before the lesson to ensure that the blocks are frozen solid.

1. Gather two bowls—a large mixing bowl and a small cereal bowl.

2. Line each bowl with plastic wrap. Completely cover the inside of each bowl, letting the extra wrap drape down the sides.

3. Fill each bowl ¾ full of water.

4. Drape half of a 1-foot length of string into each bowl. When the water freezes, you will need to be able to pull the ice block with the string, so allow some length for doing so.

5. Freeze the water overnight, or until it is solid.

Keywords and Pronunciation

kilogram: A metric unit of mass. The stone weighs 5 grams.

mass: The amount of matter in an object. The resistance of an object to a change in its motion. The mass of an object stays the same whether the object is on Earth or on the moon.

mass balance: A tool that measures mass, sometimes just called a balance. We used the mass balance to find the mass of the toy.

spring scale: A tool that measures weight. We weighed the coins with the spring scale.

weight: The pull of gravity on an object. The weight of the apple was more than the weight of the egg.

LEARN

Activity 1: Understanding Mass and Weight *(Online)*

Activity 2: Experimenting with Mass *(Offline)*

Line the two bowls with plastic wrap that covers the entire bowl and drapes down the sides. Fill both bowls ¾ full of water. Drape half of a 1-foot length of string into the bowl. When frozen, you will need to be able to pull the ice block with the string, so allow some length for doing so. Freeze overnight, or until solid.

1. Carefully coat the bottom surface of the bathtub with a light layer of baby oil.

2. Remove the blocks of ice from their bowls, using the plastic wrap to help you pull out each block in a single chunk.

3. Lay both ice blocks on the bathtub surface that has been slightly covered with baby oil.

4. Hold the string of the smaller ice block and pull it across the bathtub surface. Was it easy to get it moving?

5. Repeat the process with the larger ice block.

Which was easier to get moving, the smaller ice block or the larger ice block? Which ice block is more massive? Which ice block is less massive?

Experiment with how much force is needed to get each ice block up to the same speed. That depends on how massive the object is. The more mass it has, the more force is required to get it going.

Note that gravity may make the ice blocks start to move on their own because bathtubs aren't always very level! This shouldn't affect your experiment—you should still be able to feel the difference in how hard it is to change the motion of the ice blocks.

Line the two bowls with plastic wrap that covers the entire bowl and drapes down the sides. Fill both bowls ¾ full of water. Drape half of a 1-foot length of string into the bowl. When frozen, you will need to be able to pull the ice block with the string, so allow some length for doing so. Freeze overnight, or until solid.

1. Carefully coat the bottom surface of the bathtub with a light layer of baby oil.

2. Remove the blocks of ice from their bowls, using the plastic wrap to help you pull out each block in a single chunk.

3. Lay both ice blocks on the bathtub surface that has been slightly covered with baby oil.

4. Hold the string of the smaller ice block and pull it across the bathtub surface. Was it easy to get it moving?

5. Repeat the process with the larger ice block.

Which was easier to get moving, the smaller ice block or the larger ice block? Which ice block is more massive? Which ice block is less massive?

Experiment with how much force is needed to get each ice block up to the same speed. That depends on how massive the object is. The more mass it has, the more force is required to get it going.

Note that gravity may make the ice blocks start to move on their own because bathtubs aren't always very level! This shouldn't affect your experiment—you should still be able to feel the difference in how hard it is to change the motion of the ice blocks.

Safety

The bathtub will be very slippery. Don't allow student to stand in the tub until you've thoroughly washed it with soap and water.

ASSESS

Lesson Assessment: Mass and Weight (*Online*)

You will complete an online assessment covering the main objectives of the lesson.

LEARN

Activity 3: What Do You Weigh on Jupiter? (*Online*)

Activity 4: Optional: ZlugQuest Measurement (*Online*)

Student Guide

Magnets

Magnets attract or repel other magnets. Magnets use forces that can even push or pull objects without touching them! In this lesson, you will learn about how magnets interact with other magnets and certain kinds of metals.

Lesson Objectives

- Ask questions to determine a cause-and-effect relationship of electric or magnetic interactions between two objects not in contact with each other.
- Define a simple design problem that can be solved by applying scientific ideas about magnets.

PREPARE

Approximate lesson time is 60 minutes.

Materials

For the Student

    2 magnets

    Magnet Assignment

LEARN

Activity 1: Magnetic Physical Properties *(Online)*

Activity 2: Lesson Review *(Online)*

ASSESS

Lesson Assessment: Adapting to Change *(Offline)*

Sit with an adult to review the assessment questions.

Name _____ Date _____

Assignment

Magnets

Use two magnets to discover properties of magnets.

Activity 1

1. Use one magnet and test different metals in and around your home. Which metal objects are attracted to the magnet? Test the items and record your observations.

Metallic Object	Attracted	Not Attracted
refrigerator		
doorknob		
nail		
paper clip		
water faucet		

2. What can you conclude about the metal that the magnet was attracted to?

_____

_____

_____

_____

Activity 2

Use your two magnets to determine which poles attract and which poles repel. You can label one side of each magnet north and the other side south if they do not already have labels. Use your magnets to answer the following questions.

3. Ask a question about the relationship between north and north poles on magnets that are not touching. Then, answer your question.

   _____

   _____

   _____

   _____

4. Ask a question about the relationship between north and south poles on magnets that are not touching. Then, answer your question.

   _____

   _____

   _____

   _____

Student Guide

Matter and Engineering

How good are you at solving problems? How good are you at designing a solution to solve a problem? There is a process to follow that helps guide you through solving a problem. You will be given a problem to solve using your understanding of magnets. Let's get started!

Lesson Objectives

- Define a simple design problem that can be solved by applying scientific ideas about magnets.
- Define a simple design problem reflecting a need or a want that includes specified criteria for success and constraints on materials, time, or cost.
- Generate or compare multiple possible solutions to a problem based on how well each is likely to meet the criteria and constraints of the problem.

PREPARE

Approximate lesson time is 60 minutes.

Materials

For the Student

Design a Solution Graded Assignment

LEARN

Activity 1: Design Process *(Online)*

Activity 2: Find a Solution *(Online)*

Activity 3: Lesson Review *(Online)*

Name _____ Date _____

Graded Assignment

Design a Solution

Use two magnets to discover properties of magnets.

Total score: _____ of 20 points

This assignment will require you to use the design process in order to solve a problem using magnets.

> **Situation**: After weeks of work, you and your mother have finished building a tree house. Your mom tells you to put the toolbox back in the garage. Before you know it, you trip over the edge of a sandbox! All the iron nails are sent flying into the sandbox that your little brother is playing in. Your brother wasn't hurt, but the nails are lost. Use the design process to come up with a solution.

1. **Define the problem**. This step is to make sure that you focus on one specific problem. When you define a problem, you come up with a statement about what the problem is. Keep the statement clear and to the point.

   _____

   _____

   _____

   _____

2. **Define criteria for the solution**. This means that you figure out the different parts of a solution that fix the problem. Whatever the solution is, it needs to meet certain goals.

   _____

   _____

   _____

   _____

3. **Describe some constraints for the design.** Constraints are limitations to a design. Time and money are typical constraints. This step is to try and figure out and work around problems and be prepared. It would be great to have unlimited resources, but that rarely happens in real life. As a student, one of your constraints would be that you are only using household items.

_____

_____

_____

_____

4. **Describe possible solutions.** Briefly write out two or three plans that will solve the problem.

_____

_____

_____

_____

5. **Analyze the possible solutions to determine which solution will work best.** Look at each solution as if it is new to you. Try and think of a reason why each solution might not work and record your thoughts. Then choose the strongest option.

_____

_____

_____

_____

6. **Build and test one of the solutions (on a small scale)**. Think about the solution you decided on from Step 5. Now, think about the items you have around your house that can be used to make your design. Create your design. Now, put together a test for this design and try it out.

_____

_____

_____

_____

7. **Analyze the results of the test**. Look at the results from you test. Was your device successful? What did you learn from the test? What problems or failure points came up?

_____

_____

_____

_____

8. **Suggest improvements based on the analysis**. Think about the problems or failure points that came up during your analysis. Write down suggestions to improve the device based on the analysis.

_____

_____

_____

_____

Student Guide

Matter and Engineering: Design

Now that you have your design problem it is time to brainstorm solutions. Be creative when you come up with solutions. After you have a few good ones, you will need to analyze each one and decide on the strongest solution.

Lesson Objectives

- Define a simple design problem that can be solved by applying scientific ideas about magnets.
- Define a simple design problem reflecting a need or a want that includes specified criteria for success and constraints on materials, time, or cost.
- Generate or compare multiple possible solutions to a problem based on how well each is likely to meet the criteria and constraints of the problem.

PREPARE

Approximate lesson time is 60 minutes.

Materials

For the Student

Design a Solution Graded Assignment

LEARN

Activity 1: Brainstorming Solutions *(Online)*

Activity 2: Lesson Review *(Online)*

Name _____   Date _____

Graded Assignment

Design a Solution

Use two magnets to discover properties of magnets.

Total score: _____ of 20 points

This assignment will require you to use the design process in order to solve a problem using magnets.

> **Situation**: After weeks of work, you and your mother have finished building a tree house. Your mom tells you to put the toolbox back in the garage. Before you know it, you trip over the edge of a sandbox! All the iron nails are sent flying into the sandbox that your little brother is playing in. Your brother wasn't hurt, but the nails are lost. Use the design process to come up with a solution.

1. **Define the problem**. This step is to make sure that you focus on one specific problem. When you define a problem, you come up with a statement about what the problem is. Keep the statement clear and to the point.

   _____

   _____

   _____

   _____

2. **Define criteria for the solution**. This means that you figure out the different parts of a solution that fix the problem. Whatever the solution is, it needs to meet certain goals.

   _____

   _____

   _____

   _____

3. **Describe some constraints for the design**. Constraints are limitations to a design. Time and money are typical constraints. This step is to try and figure out and work around problems and be prepared. It would be great to have unlimited resources, but that rarely happens in real life. As a student, one of your constraints would be that you are only using household items.

_____

_____

_____

_____

4. **Describe possible solutions**. Briefly write out two or three plans that will solve the problem.

_____

_____

_____

_____

5. **Analyze the possible solutions to determine which solution will work best**. Look at each solution as if it is new to you. Try and think of a reason why each solution might not work and record your thoughts. Then choose the strongest option.

_____

_____

_____

_____

6. **Build and test one of the solutions (on a small scale).** Think about the solution you decided on from Step 5. Now, think about the items you have around your house that can be used to make your design. Create your design. Now, put together a test for this design and try it out.

_____

_____

_____

_____

7. **Analyze the results of the test.** Look at the results from you test. Was your device successful? What did you learn from the test? What problems or failure points came up?

_____

_____

_____

_____

8. **Suggest improvements based on the analysis.** Think about the problems or failure points that came up during your analysis. Write down suggestions to improve the device based on the analysis.

_____

_____

_____

_____

Student Guide
Matter and Engineering: Testing

Now that you have your design problem, it is time to brainstorm solutions. Be creative when you come up with solutions. After you have a few good ones, you will need to analyze each one and decide on the strongest solution.

Lesson Objectives

- Define a simple design problem that can be solved by applying scientific ideas about magnets.
- Define a simple design problem reflecting a need or a want that includes specified criteria for success and constraints on materials, time, or cost.
- Generate or compare multiple possible solutions to a problem based on how well each is likely to meet the criteria and constraints of the problem.
- Plan and carry out fair tests in which variables are controlled and failure points are considered to identify aspects of a model or prototype that can be improved.

PREPARE

Approximate lesson time is 60 minutes.

Materials

For the Student

Design a Solution Graded Assignment

Keywords and Pronunciation

control variable: A factor that will not change during an experiment; also known as a constant

independent variable: In an experiment, the factor that a scientist deliberately changes

LEARN

Activity 1: Testing and Improvement *(Online)*

Activity 2: Planning it Out *(Online)*

Activity 3: Lesson Review *(Online)*

Name _____ Date _____

Graded Assignment

Design a Solution

Use two magnets to discover properties of magnets.

Total score: _____ of 20 points

This assignment will require you to use the design process in order to solve a problem using magnets.

> **Situation**: After weeks of work, you and your mother have finished building a tree house. Your mom tells you to put the toolbox back in the garage. Before you know it, you trip over the edge of a sandbox! All the iron nails are sent flying into the sandbox that your little brother is playing in. Your brother wasn't hurt, but the nails are lost. Use the design process to come up with a solution.

1. **Define the problem**. This step is to make sure that you focus on one specific problem. When you define a problem, you come up with a statement about what the problem is. Keep the statement clear and to the point.

   _____

   _____

   _____

   _____

2. **Define criteria for the solution**. This means that you figure out the different parts of a solution that fix the problem. Whatever the solution is, it needs to meet certain goals.

   _____

   _____

   _____

   _____

3. **Describe some constraints for the design**. Constraints are limitations to a design. Time and money are typical constraints. This step is to try and figure out and work around problems and be prepared. It would be great to have unlimited resources, but that rarely happens in real life. As a student, one of your constraints would be that you are only using household items.

_____

_____

_____

_____

4. **Describe possible solutions**. Briefly write out two or three plans that will solve the problem.

_____

_____

_____

_____

5. **Analyze the possible solutions to determine which solution will work best**. Look at each solution as if it is new to you. Try and think of a reason why each solution might not work and record your thoughts. Then choose the strongest option.

_____

_____

_____

_____

6. **Build and test one of the solutions (on a small scale)**. Think about the solution you decided on from Step 5. Now, think about the items you have around your house that can be used to make your design. Create your design. Now, put together a test for this design and try it out.

_____

_____

_____

_____

7. **Analyze the results of the test**. Look at the results from you test. Was your device successful? What did you learn from the test? What problems or failure points came up?

_____

_____

_____

_____

8. **Suggest improvements based on the analysis**. Think about the problems or failure points that came up during your analysis. Write down suggestions to improve the device based on the analysis.

_____

_____

_____

_____

Student Guide

Properties of Matter: Unit Review and Assessment

Can you identify the three states of matter? How does matter change when heated or cooled? Test your knowledge on the properties of matter in this Unit Review.

Lesson Objectives

- Recognize that *mass* is a measure of the resistance of an object to acceleration by a force.
- Convert measurements from one metric unit to another one of the same dimensions, such as mm to cm.
- Demonstrate mastery of the knowledge and skills taught in this unit.
- Describe how matter changes state when heated (solid to liquid to gas) or cooled (gas to liquid to solid).
- Describe the motion of atoms in solids, liquids, and gases (atoms in solids vibrate but do not move around; atoms in liquids move around but stay close to other atoms; and atoms in gases move freely).
- Describe the properties of solids, liquids, and gases (solids have a definite shape and a definite volume; liquids have a definite volume but no definite shape; gases have neither a definite shape nor a definite volume).
- Identify three states of matter: solid, liquid, and gas.
- Recognize that all matter is made of particles called *atoms,* much too small to see with the naked eye and constantly in motion.
- Recognize that the mass of an object stays the same, but the object's weight varies depending on where the object is being weighed.
- Recognize that *volume* is the amount of space occupied by matter, or the amount of space inside a container.
- Use appropriate tools to measure the length, volume, mass, and weight of different objects in metric units.
- Define *volume* as the amount of space occupied by matter, or the amount of space inside a container.
- Describe how matter changes states by freezing, melting, or boiling when heated.
- Recognize that *mass* is a measure of the resistance of an object to acceleration by a force.
- Recognize that the mass of an object stays the same, but the object's weight changes depending on where in the universe the object is being weighed.
- Use appropriate tools to measure in metric units the length, volume, mass, and weight of different objects.
- Compare the motion of atoms in solids, liquids, and gases (atoms in solids vibrate around a fixed position, atoms in liquids do not stay in a fixed position but remain close to each other, and atoms in gases move freely, bouncing off other atoms but not staying close together most of the time).

- Convert measurements from centimeters to millimeters.
- Describe properties of solids, liquids, and gases (for example, solids have a definite shape and a definite volume; liquids have a definite volume but no definite shape; gases have neither a definite shape nor a definite volume).
- Recognize that all matter is made up of particles called *atoms,* which are much too small to see with the naked eye and are constantly in motion.

PREPARE

Approximate lesson time is 60 minutes.

Advance Preparation

- Your student will review the properties of matter by making a simple gelatin recipe. Before the lesson, you will need to purchase a 4-serving package of gelatin dessert mix, and some club soda or carbonated fruit drink. You will also need a 9" x 13" glass baking dish or gelatin mold.
- Your student will measure her ingredients. Clean the metric ruler and graduated cylinder thoroughly before using them to measure food.

Materials

For the Student

Properties of Matter Unit Review

LEARN

Activity 1: Properties of Matter Unit Review (Offline)

Safety

Never leave your student unattended near a stove, oven, or microwave.

This lesson involves eating or working with food. Check with your doctor, if necessary, to find out whether your student will have any allergic reaction to the food.

ASSESS

Unit Assessment: Properties of Matter (Offline)

Complete an offline Unit Assessment. Your learning coach will score the assessment.

LEARN

Activity 2: Optional: ZlugQuest Measurement (Online)

Name _____   Date _____

Properties of Matter
Unit Review

Put your knowledge of the properties of matter to the test, and see what can happen when you combine different types of matter.

Part 1 – What's the Matter?

1. Matter exists in three states, _____, _____, and _____.

| A | B | C |

2.

Look at the three cups illustrated above. How would you describe the matter in each cup? Choose from these terms: definite shape, no definite shape, definite volume, no definite volume.

Cup A

_____

Cup B (bubbles only)

_____

Cup C

_____

3. The matter in Cup A is in a _____ state.
4. The matter in Cup B is in a _____ state.
5. The matter in Cup C is in a _____ state.

6. Did any of the cups have properties of more than one state of matter? Explain.

_____

_____

_____

7. Look at the bubble rising to the surface in Cup B. What kind of matter is inside the bubbles in Cup B?

_____

8. What happens to this matter when the bubbles pop?

_____

Measure It

9. What tool measures volume?

_____

10. What is the volume of the matter in Cup C? (Remember to write the units.)

_____

11. Mass is the amount of _____ in an object.

12. What tool measures mass?

_____

13. What tool measures weight?

_____

14. If you had a weight scale of some kind, you could weigh the material in Cup C with it. Would the matter in Cup C have the same mass on the moon?

_____

15. Would it have the same weight on the moon? Why?

_____

_____

_____

Watch It Change

Have an adult guide you through this activity.

16. Pour the matter from Cup C into a pot and heat it. Watch as the matter in Cup C heats to a boil. When a liquid is heated, it becomes a

_____

17. All matter is made of atoms. What is happening when a liquid changes to a gas?

_____

18. Mix the gelatin into the pot and then pour the mixture from the pot into a bowl. Watch as an adult mixes the matter from Cup B into the bowl. The watch as Cup A is added to the mixture. When a solid is heated, it changes

_____

19. Measure the length of the pan that you will pour the mixture into. How long is it in centimeters?

_____

20. Without measuring the pan again, how long is it in millimeters?

_____

21. Pour the mixture into the pan. Cover the pan with plastic wrap and put it in the refrigerator. Let it set for 30 minutes. Look at the droplets on the plastic wrap. The matter became a gas, then cooled and became a

_____

22. The mixture in the bowl was a liquid. When a liquid is cooled, it becomes a

_____

Safety: Check with your doctor, if necessary, to find out whether your student will have any allergic reaction to the food.

Enjoy!

Uncover the pan, and help yourself to the changing states of matter!

Part 2 — Measure It!

Length

Find two objects around your home. Object A should have a length that can be measured in meters. Object B should fit in the neck of the graduated cylinder and be something that sinks.

There are three phases of matter: solid, liquid, and gas.

23. Look at Object A. Is it a solid, liquid, or gas?

_____

24. What properties does it have?

_____

25. Use a metric ruler to record the length of the object in meters.

_____

26. How long is it in centimeters?

_____

27. How long is it in millimeters?

_____

28. What patterns do you notice in the measurements?

_____

_____

Volume

What is volume? *Volume* is the amount of space occupied by matter, or the amount of space inside a container. You can find the volume of Object B by using the graduated cylinder.

Fill the graduated cylinder with 50 mL of water.

Carefully place Object B in the graduated cylinder.

29. To what level did the water rise?

_____

30. Subtract the original 50 mL of water from the new water level

_____

This difference tells how much space in the cylinder Object B takes up—its volume.

Teacher tip: If your student can take one measurement and do the mathematical computation to find the other measurements, have the student do so. Have the student check that calculation by measuring.

Student Guide

Physical Changes

Is a mashed apple different than a chunk of apple? It is still an apple—it has just been through a physical change. Experiment with other objects to identify physical changes when the objects are cut, broken, or change phases.

Lesson Objectives

- Describe a *physical change of matter* as a change in size and shape (through cutting, breaking, or grinding), or state (through melting, boiling, freezing, evaporating, or condensing).
- Recognize that a physical change does not change the molecules that make up matter.

PREPARE

Approximate lesson time is 60 minutes.

Advance Preparation

- For this lesson, you will need 1 cup of trail mix and a bowlful of salad to demonstrate that items in mixtures have the same physical properties in or outside of the mixture. Purchase or create mixtures that have a good variety of items that easily can be sorted by type (for example, carrots, cucumbers, lettuce, and grape tomatoes).

Keywords and Pronunciation

physical change: A change in matter from one form to another without becoming a new substance. When water freezes and turns to ice it goes through a physical change, but it is still water.

physical property: A characteristic of an object based on its size, shape, color, and state of matter. A physical property of some apples is that they are red.

LEARN

Activity 1: What Is a Physical Change? *(Online)*

Activity 2: Mixtures *(Offline)*

A box of crayons, a salad, and a cup of trail mix all are mixtures. The parts of a mixture have undergone a physical change when they mix with other parts, but each part keeps its own properties.

1. Remove the crayons from the box.

2. Sort them according to groups. You may choose to sort them according to similar shades, size, or by primary and secondary colors. You decide!

3. Look at each group. Can we still call them crayons even though they are not all together in the box? [1] Did their physical properties change when you took them out of the box? [2]

4. Place the cup of trail mix on the table. It is a mixture, too. Separate the mixture into its parts. For example, if there are peanuts in your mixture, place them all in a group together. Place raisins in a group of their own, as well as any other item.

5. Did the properties of the nuts and raisins change when you separated them from the whole? [3]

6. Next, place the salad on the table. Like the trail mix, it is a mixture. Separate the parts of the mixture so that you have a group that represents each item in the salad. Look at each group. Did any of their properties change when you separated them from the whole salad? [4]

Safety

This lesson involves working with food. Before starting, check with your doctor, if necessary, to find out whether your student will have any allergic reactions.

Activity 3: Was That a Physical Change? *(Offline)*

1. Fill a graduated cylinder with 100 mL of water. Pour it into a clear drinking glass.

2. Fill the graduated cylinder again with 100 mL of water and add it to the glass.

3. Use the graduated cylinder to measure 10 mL of salt. Add it to the 200 mL of water in the clear drinking glass.

4. Stir the salt and water mixture with a spoon. What do you observe happening in the glass?

5. Carefully pour the saltwater mixture into a pan. Place the pan on the stove and set it on high heat to boil.

6. Watch the water in the pan as it boils and eventually evaporates. This may take 5 to 10 minutes, depending on the size of the pan.

7. Caution: Watch the pot carefully as the last liquid boils away. Take the pot off the stove right away to avoid overheating the pot!

Look carefully at the bottom of the pan. What do you see? [1]

IMPORTANT! Set aside the pan until it has cooled completely.

Wet your finger and rub it on the bottom of the pan. Now lick your finger.

How does it taste? [2] What do you think that white coating in the pan is? [3]

A *solution* is a mixture in which one element has dissolved into the other. Saltwater is a solution. The crystals seem to vanish in the water, but boiling the solution will cause them to reappear.

As with mixtures, you can separate the substances that make up solutions. The properties of the water and the salt in the pan did not change.

If you want: use a magnifying glass to look at the particles at the bottom of the pan, and notice their shape. Compare with the salt from a salt shaker. What do you see?

Safety

Never leave your student unattended near a stove or oven and working with boiling water.

ASSESS

Lesson Assessment: Physical Changes *(Online)*

You will complete an online assessment covering the main objectives of this lesson. Your assessment will be scored by the computer.

Student Guide

Chemical Changes

A rusty bike? A toasted marshmallow? A burnt piece of wood? Have these objects gone through chemical or physical changes? Investigate the answers in several experiments.

Lesson Objectives

- Classify changes of matter as chemical or physical.
- Identify clues that suggest a chemical change (for example, a color change, a change in temperature, or the production of light).
- Recognize that a *chemical change* occurs when atoms within molecules rearrange themselves, changing one substance into another.

PREPARE

Approximate lesson time is 60 minutes.

Materials

For the Student

Change Matters

Keywords and Pronunciation

chemical change: A change that results in the formation of one or more new substances. As the iron chair rusted, it went through a chemical change.

molecule (MAH-lih-kyool)**:** The smallest part of a substance that keeps all the properties of the substance and is composed of one or more atoms. The molecules of the sugar mixed with the molecules of the water.

substance: Matter that has particular properties. Salt is a substance that dissolves easily in water.

LEARN

Activity 1: What Is a Chemical Change? *(Online)*

Activity 2: Experiment with Chemical Changes *(Offline)*

There are two ways that matter can change—through a physical change or a chemical change. A physical change does not change a substance itself—that is, how the atoms are arranged into molecules—but it may change its size or shape.

Changes in state are also physical changes. When you boil water—a liquid—and it turns to water vapor, it has gone through a physical change. It has changed into a different state, but the substance itself has not been changed—the molecules are the same.

Some changes, however, change the substance, making something new. These are called chemical changes. Complete the experiments below to decide if the change is a physical or chemical change.

Experiment 1: Ice Cube

Remove one ice cube from the ice cube tray. Place it in a plastic cup. Observe the ice cube for a few minutes. Record your results for the Ice Cube experiment on your Changing Matter sheet.

Experiment 2: Vinegar with Steel Wool

Check the temperature of the room with a thermometer. Soak the steel wool in a cup of 15 mL of vinegar for one minute. Take the steel wool out of the cup and squeeze out any extra vinegar.

Wrap the steel wool around the thermometer and put them into the other cup. Put the lid on the cup. If needed, let the end of the thermometer stick out through the hole in the lid.Wait 5 minutes, then check the temperature on the thermometer. Compare it with the first reading.

Record your results for the Vinegar with Steel Wool experiment on your Changing Matter sheet.

Experiment 3: Baking Soda with Vinegar

Place the plastic cup on the baking sheet. Place 10 mL of baking soda into a plastic cup. You may notice a temperature change by touching the cup as you add the baking soda. Rinse out the graduated cylinder. Fill it with 50 mL of vinegar, again noting the temperature by touch. Add it to the cup and watch closely. Note any temperature changes you observe.

Record your results for the Baking Soda with Vinegar experiment on your Changing Matter sheet.

Experiment 4: Celery Stick

Carefully cut the celery stick in half. Observe the changes after a few minutes.

Record your results for the celery stick experiment on your Changing Matter sheet.

Safety

This lesson involves working with food. Check to find out whether your student will have any allergic reactions to the food. Do not let your student handle the knife.

ASSESS

Lesson Assessment: Chemical Changes (*Online*)

You will complete an online assessment covering the main objectives of the lesson.

Name _____ Date _____

Chemical Changes
Change Matters

Check off your results for each experiment. Explain your results in the last column.

Experiment	Physical Change	Chemical Change	Both	Why?
Ice Cube				
Vinegar with Steel Wool				
Baking Soda with Vinegar				
Celery Stick				

Student Guide
Atoms

Atoms? Molecules? How are they all related to make up matter? Build two models to discover the microscopic world of the atom.

Lesson Objectives

- Explain that an *element* is a substance made up of just one kind of atom, all with the same number of protons (and electrons).
- Name the three parts of an atom (protons, neutrons, and electrons).
- State that all matter is made up of particles too small to see called *atoms* which combine to form many kinds of molecules.
- Explain that several atoms, often many, bind together to form molecules. A sample of a single substance contains many identical molecules.
- Explain that the atoms of one element have different properties than the atoms of another element.

PREPARE

Approximate lesson time is 60 minutes.

Advance Preparation

- If you don't already have them, you will need large green grapes, large purple grapes, and green peas for the Make a Model Atom activity in this lesson.

Keywords and Pronunciation

atom: A tiny particle that is the fundamental building block of substances. The properties of the atom determine the properties of the element made up only of those atoms.

compound (KAHM-pownd)**:** A substance containing atoms of two or more elements. Water is a compound of hydrogen and oxygen.

electron: A tiny part of an atom with a negative electric charge. In an atom, electrons form a cloud around the nucleus.

element: A chemical substance that contains only one kind of atom and that cannot be broken down into simpler substances. Oxygen is an element.

molecule (MAH-lih-kyool)**:** The smallest bit into which a chemical substance can be divided and still have the properties of that substance. Molecules of water contain hydrogen and oxygen atoms.

neutron: A particle in the nucleus of an atom, which has no electric charge. Atoms contain neutrons, electrons, and protons.

nucleus (NOO-klee-uhs)**:** The core of an atom made up of protons and neutrons. Electrons form a cloud around the nucleus of an atom.

proton: A tiny part of the nucleus of an atom, which has a positive electric charge. The number of protons determines the chemical properties of the atom.

LEARN

Activity 1: Atoms: Building Blocks of All Matter (Online)

Activity 2: Make a Model Atom (Offline)

Let's build a model of the most common kind of oxygen atom!

1. Cut a piece of plastic wrap about 45 cm long and place it on the table.

2. Gather the 8 large, green grapes. The grapes will bete protons—the tiny part of the atoms s that have a positive electric charge. They make up part of the nucleus. Remember, the nucleus is the core of an atom that is made up of protons and neutrons. Place the 8 green grapes on the plastic wrap.

3. Gather the 8 large, purple grapes. These are the neutrons—the particles with no electric charge, and that make up part of the nucleus. Most oxygen atoms have just 8 neutrons—some have 9 or even 10 neutrons.

4. Wrap the plastic wrap tightly around the grapes so they form a ball. You have just formed the nucleus of the oxygen atom.

5. Carefully place a pea on the end of each toothpick. The peas are the electrons, the tiny parts of the atom with a negative charge. The electrons are outside the nucleus, which is why we didn't put them inside the plastic wrap with the protons and neutrons.

6. Poke the toothpicks into all sides of the nucleus so they stick out like porcupine quills.

You did it! Now review the parts of the oxygen atom.

What do the large, green grapes represent? [1]

What do the large, purple grapes represent? [2]

What do the peas on the ends of the toothpicks represent? [3]

Activity 3: Make a Model Water Molecule (Offline)

Water has a special chemical formula—H_2O. This formula shows that a water molecule contains two atoms of hydrogen and one atom of oxygen.

1. Choose different colors of clay. You will use one color to make the hydrogen atoms and the other to make the oxygen atom.

2. Make a round oxygen atom about the size of your fist. First, form the nuclues from 8 protons and 8 neutrons—like the grapes in the last activity. We can't see them, but around the outside are the 8 electrons—like the peas.

3. Use the other color clay to make two hydrogen atoms that are half the size of the oxygen atom. Make each hydrogen atom of one proton and one electron.

4. Carefully press the two hydrogen molecules on either side of the oxygen atom, looking a little like "mouse ears."

You have just made a model of H_2O, or water! The formula H_2O shows that two hydrogen atoms and one oxygen atom are joined tightly together. Each group of two hydrogen atoms and one oxygen atom is a molecule.

ASSESS

Lesson Assessment: Atoms *(Online)*

You will complete an online assessment covering the main objectives of this lesson. Your assessment will be scored by the computer.

Student Guide
Mendeleev and the Periodic Table

How many elements have scientists discovered? How are the elements organized? Explore the Periodic Table of the Elements to discover patterns and relationships between elements.

Lesson Objectives

- Locate elements on the periodic table.
- Identify Dimitry Mendeleev as the scientist who first successfully arranged all the known chemical elements into a table according to their common properties.
- Identify the chemical symbols of the four common elements that make up living things: carbon, oxygen, nitrogen, and hydrogen.
- Recognize that elements are represented by chemical symbols.

PREPARE

Approximate lesson time is 60 minutes.

Materials

For the Student

    Let's Search the Periodic Table

Keywords and Pronunciation

atom: The smallest part of an element that affects its chemical behavior. Atoms make up molecules.

Dimitry Mendeleev (dih-MEE-tree men-duh-LAY-uhf)

element: a material composed of one kind of atom, with a fixed number of protons in its nucleus; elements combine to form many kinds of matter

Jons Jacob Berzilius (youns YAH-kawp buhr-ZAY-lee-uhs)

periodic table: An organized chart of all known elements. Mendeleev organized elements into the periodic table.

LEARN

Activity 1: The Periodic Table of the Elements *(Online)*

Activity 2: Learn Your Way Around the Periodic Table *(Offline)*

Let's look at one element—hydrogen. You can find hydrogen in the first box in the upper left-hand corner. Its name is at the top of the box. There is a capital H in the box as well. H is the symbol for hydrogen. Each element has a symbol that is unique. No two elements have the same symbol.

The number 1 below the element name stands for the element's atomic number. Each element has a different atomic number. This number shows the number of protons in the element. Protons are the positively charged particles found in the nucleus.

All the known elements are arranged into this table, which works a lot like a calendar. Think about a calendar that shows one month at a time. The date of each day increases as you move from left to right across the rows and from the top to the bottom. The periodic table works the same way.

Now find carbon on the periodic table. Here's a hint—its symbol is C.

Where is carbon located? [1]

What is its atomic number? [2]

ASSESS

Lesson Assessment: Mendeleev and the Periodic Table (*Online*)

You will complete an online assessment covering the main objectives of the lesson.

LEARN

Activity 3: The Periodic Table Comes Alive (*Online*)

Safety

As always, you may wish to preview any websites before your student views them.

Name _____   Date _____

Mendeleev and the Periodic Table
Let's Search the Periodic Table

Let's search the periodic table for more information about the elements.

1. Find nitrogen on the periodic table. What is its symbol?

    _____

    What is its atomic number?

    _____

2. Find the element that is represented by the symbol O. What is the name of this element?

    _____

    What is its atomic number?

    _____

3. List some elements that have a one-letter symbol that is also the first letter of the word.

    _____

    _____

4. Find two elements that have a symbol that is entirely different from the spelling of the word.

    _____

    Do you remember why they might have names like this?

    _____

5. Find two elements that are named after planets.

    _____

You have learned about a few of the elements on the periodic table. Let's look back at four of them: carbon, nitrogen, oxygen, and hydrogen. They are very common on earth and inside our bodies. Carbon is the main building block of the compounds that make up our bodies. Green plants separate oxygen from the carbon dioxide in the air, and animals use it to breathe. Nitrogen makes up most of the air. Our bodies need nitrogen to make proteins. Hydrogen is one of the elements, along with oxygen, that joins to form water, a necessity for all of life.

Name _____   Date _____

The Periodic Table of Elements

hydrogen 1 H																	helium 2 He
lithium 3 Li	beryllium 4 Be											boron 5 B	carbon 6 C	nitrogen 7 N	oxygen 8 O	fluorine 9 F	neon 10 Ne
sodium 11 Na	magnesium 12 Mg											aluminum 13 Al	silicon 14 Si	phosphorus 15 P	sulfur 16 S	chlorine 17 Cl	argon 18 Ar
potassium 19 K	calcium 20 Ca	scandium 21 Sc	titanium 22 Ti	vanadium 23 V	chromium 24 Cr	manganese 25 Mn	iron 26 Fe	cobalt 27 Co	nickel 28 Ni	copper 29 Cu	zinc 30 Zn	gallium 31 Ga	germanium 32 Ge	arsenic 33 As	selenium 34 Se	bromine 35 Br	krypton 36 Kr
rubidium 37 Rb	strontium 38 Sr	yttrium 39 Y	zirconium 40 Zr	niobium 41 Nb	molybdenum 42 Mo	technetium 43 Tc	ruthenium 44 Ru	rhodium 45 Rh	palladium 46 Pd	silver 47 Ag	cadmium 48 Cd	indium 49 In	tin 50 Sn	antimony 51 Sb	tellurium 52 Te	iodine 53 I	xenon 54 Xe
cesium 55 Cs	barium 56 Ba	lutetium 71 Lu	hafnium 72 Hf	tantalum 73 Ta	tungsten 74 W	rhenium 75 Re	osmium 76 Os	iridium 77 Ir	platinum 78 Pt	gold 79 Au	mercury 80 Hg	thallium 81 Tl	lead 82 Pb	bismuth 83 Bi	polonium 84 Po	astatine 85 At	radon 86 Rn
francium 87 Fr	radium 88 Ra	lawrencium 103 Lr	rutherfordium 104 Rf	dubnium 105 Db	seaborgium 106 Sg	bohrium 107 Bh	hassium 108 Hs	meitnerium 109 Mt	ununnilium 110 Uun	unununium 111 Uuu	ununbium 112 Uub	ununtrium	ununquadium 114 Uuq		ununhexium 116 Uuh		ununoctium 118 Uuo

lanthanum 57 La	cerium 58 Ce	praseodymium 59 Pr	neodymium 60 Nd	promethium 61 Pm	samarium 62 Sm	europium 63 Eu	gadolinium 64 Gd	terbium 65 Tb	dysprosium 66 Dy	holmium 67 Ho	erbium 68 Er	thulium 69 Tm	ytterbium 70 Yb
actinium 89 Ac	thorium 90 Th	protactinium 91 Pa	uranium 92 U	neptunium 93 Np	plutonium 94 Pu	americium 95 Am	curium 96 Cm	berkelium 97 Bk	californium 98 Cf	einsteinium 99 Es	fermium 100 Fm	mendelevium 101 Md	nobelium 102 No

Student Guide
Physical and Chemical Changes of Matter:
Unit Review and Assessment

Review and demonstrate what you have learned about physical and chemical changes.

Lesson Objectives

- Demonstrate mastery of the important knowledge and skills taught in this unit.

PREPARE

Approximate lesson time is 60 minutes.

Materials

For the Student

Periodic Table of the Elements

LEARN

Activity 1: Unit Review *(Online)*

Activity 2: Hands-On Review *(Offline)*

Part 1:

1. Take a quarter-stick of butter or margarine from its wrapper.

2. What could you do to the object that would cause a physical change?

3. Let's try a few. First, cut the stick of butter in two. You have just changed its size. That's a physical change.

4. Next, place one of the parts into a pan on the stove. Add a little heat and watch what happens in a few minutes. Melting the stick of butter changes its shape and its state. It was once a solid, but when heat was added it changed to a liquid.

5. Wait until the butter starts to bubble a little at the edges. Now put a piece of bread on the butter and turn the heat up a little. You will see the butter turn brown at the edges, and if you turn the bread over after one minute, you will see the bread has also turned brown. The color change strongly suggests you are seeing a chemical reaction. Ask your student to describe what happened to the bread when the heat was turned up. Have him explain the type of reaction that has taken place.

6. Turn off the heat and let the pan cool all the way down, but don't clean it yet. Explain to your student that in the center of the pan is a mixture of once-more solid butter and bread crumbs.

A chemical change tends to produce heat or light, or make new substances like the brown part of toast. A physical change does not usually do these things.

Part 2:

The periodic table is an organized chart of all the known elements. Each element is placed in its own square on the table along with its name, symbol, and atomic number. The atomic number of each element tells us the number of protons found in the nucleus of the atom. Neutrons are also part of the nucleus, but electrons are outside the nucleus. Let's review this by building a fun model of the element boron.

1. Choose one color gumdrop to be the electrons, another to be the protons, and the remaining color to be the neutrons.

2. Tear a one-foot length of plastic wrap. Lay it on the table.

3. Boron has an atomic number of five, which means there are five protons in the nucleus. The most common type of boron atom has six neutrons in the nucleus too. Place five gumdrops of one color and six of another color in the center of the plastic wrap. Gather the plastic wrap around the 11 gumdrops to form the nucleus.

4. Place one gumdrop of the third color on the end of the toothpick. Repeat until all five gumdrops are placed on the ends of separate toothpicks.

5. Carefully stick the toothpicks into the plastic wrap. Try to distribute them evenly around the nucleus.

How many protons are in the nucleus?[1] How many neutrons?[2] How many electrons circle the atom?[3] Don't forget that your model is only a model! In a real atom, the nucleus would be much, much, smaller than the electron cloud. If the electron cloud were as big as the entire solar system, the nucleus would be smaller than the Sun!

Part 3:

Let's search for some elements on the periodic table. Can you find carbon? What is its symbol?[4] What is its atomic number? [5]

Now look for hydrogen, oxygen and nitrogen. Can you name their symbols? Atomic numbers?

Safety

Keep child away from the stove when in use.

ASSESS

Unit Assessment: Physical and Chemical Changes of Matter (*Online*)

You will complete an online Unit Assessment covering the main objectives of the unit.

Name _____   Date _____

The Periodic Table of Elements

hydrogen 1 H																	helium 2 He
lithium 3 Li	beryllium 4 Be										boron 5 B	carbon 6 C	nitrogen 7 N	oxygen 8 O	fluorine 9 F	neon 10 Ne
sodium 11 Na	magnesium 12 Mg										aluminum 13 Al	silicon 14 Si	phosphorus 15 P	sulfur 16 S	chlorine 17 Cl	argon 18 Ar
potassium 19 K	calcium 20 Ca	scandium 21 Sc	titanium 22 Ti	vanadium 23 V	chromium 24 Cr	manganese 25 Mn	iron 26 Fe	cobalt 27 Co	nickel 28 Ni	copper 29 Cu	zinc 30 Zn	gallium 31 Ga	germanium 32 Ge	arsenic 33 As	selenium 34 Se	bromine 35 Br	krypton 36 Kr
rubidium 37 Rb	strontium 38 Sr	yttrium 39 Y	zirconium 40 Zr	niobium 41 Nb	molybdenum 42 Mo	technetium 43 Tc	ruthenium 44 Ru	rhodium 45 Rh	palladium 46 Pd	silver 47 Ag	cadmium 48 Cd	indium 49 In	tin 50 Sn	antimony 51 Sb	tellurium 52 Te	iodine 53 I	xenon 54 Xe
cesium 55 Cs	barium 56 Ba	lutetium 71 Lu	hafnium 72 Hf	tantalum 73 Ta	tungsten 74 W	rhenium 75 Re	osmium 76 Os	iridium 77 Ir	platinum 78 Pt	gold 79 Au	mercury 80 Hg	thallium 81 Tl	lead 82 Pb	bismuth 83 Bi	polonium 84 Po	astatine 85 At	radon 86 Rn
francium 87 Fr	radium 88 Ra	lawrencium 103 Lr	rutherfordium 104 Rf	dubnium 105 Db	seaborgium 106 Sg	bohrium 107 Bh	hassium 108 Hs	meitnerium 109 Mt	ununnilium 110 Uun	unununium 111 Uuu	ununbium 112 Uub		ununquadium 114 Uuq		ununhexium 116 Uuh		ununoctium 118 Uuo

lanthanum 57 La	cerium 58 Ce	praseodymium 59 Pr	neodymium 60 Nd	promethium 61 Pm	samarium 62 Sm	europium 63 Eu	gadolinium 64 Gd	terbium 65 Tb	dysprosium 66 Dy	holmium 67 Ho	erbium 68 Er	thulium 69 Tm	ytterbium 70 Yb
actinium 89 Ac	thorium 90 Th	protactinium 91 Pa	uranium 92 U	neptunium 93 Np	plutonium 94 Pu	americium 95 Am	curium 96 Cm	berkelium 97 Bk	californium 98 Cf	einsteinium 99 Es	fermium 100 Fm	mendelevium 101 Md	nobelium 102 No

Student Guide

Optional: Pressure

This unit is OPTIONAL. It is provided for students who seek enrichment or extra practice.

We come across many types of forces that involve fluids. Air pressure is the force of air molecules pressing on our bodies. Airplanes experience drag and thrust, as well as gravity and lift. A ship floats due to the forces of gravity and the buoyant force of water. By focusing on these forces in fluids, we can make sense of many phenomena we see around us.

You'll be amazed to find out that the air that you move very easily through is actually putting a lot of pressure on you. There is air pressure everywhere on Earth. Learn to calculate pressure. Then find out how to crush an aluminum can without touching it! Use what you know about pressure to explain the scientific reasoning behind this old favorite science "trick."

Lesson Objectives

- . Describe the forces present in flight: lift, weight, thrust, and drag.
- Explain that atmospheric pressure decreases with height above sea level and water pressure increases with depth below sea level.
- State that a substance that flows—for example, a gas or a liquid—is a *fluid*.
- Define pressure as the force exerted on a surface and recognize that pressure is measured in a unit called the pascal.

PREPARE

Approximate lesson time is 60 minutes.

Materials

For the Student

Can Crusher: It's No Trick!
baking dish, rectangular - or shallow pie plate
can - empty soda
oven mitt - or tongs
heat source - stove or hot plate
water - cold
Make a Barometer
clay
plastic bottle - 473 mL
bowl
eyedropper
food coloring
markers - permanent
ruler
straw, drinking
water

Keywords and Pronunciation

aneroid (A-nuh-royd)

barometer (buh-RAH-muh-tuhr)

Blaise Pascal (blez pahs-KAHL)

fluid: Any substance that flows. Air flows, so air is considered a fluid.

pascal (pahs-KAHL): A unit of pressure calculated by dividing the force in newtons by the area measured in square meters. Air pressure is measured in pascals.

pressure: The force acting over a given area of a surface. Even though you may not feel it, the air around you is applying pressure on you and everything around you.

LEARN

Activity 1: Optional: Lesson Instructions (*Online*)

This lesson is OPTIONAL. It is provided for students who seek enrichment or extra practice. You may skip this OPTIONAL lesson.

Please make this lesson complete in order to proceed to the next lesson in the course.

This lesson is OPTIONAL. It is provided for students who seek enrichment or extra practice. You may skip this lesson.

If you choose to skip this lesson, then go to the Plan or Lesson Lists page and mark this lesson "Skipped" in order to proceed to the next lesson in the course.

Activity 2: Optional: Fluids Put the Pressure On (*Online*)

Activity 3: Optional: Can Crusher (*Offline*)

You might be fooled by magic tricks like this can-crusher activity. But if you're up on your knowledge of pressure, you'll be able to figure out the science fact behind the "trick."

Safety

Never leave your student unattended near a stove, oven, or microwave. Use extreme caution when working with boiling water. Never leave your student unattended near hot or boiling water.

Activity 4: Optional: Make a Barometer (*Offline*)

Air pressure gives clues to changes in weather. Low pressure may mean a stormy day, while high pressure may mean bright sunlight. A *barometer* is a tool used to measure air pressure. Make a barometer and see what you can find out about the relationship between air pressure and weather changes.

Name _____   Date _____

Pressure

Can Crusher: It's No Trick!

Because air and water are fluids, their molecules flow around and bounce into things. Those moving molecules push in all directions, creating pressure.

How are air and water molecules different? Liquid molecules like those in water are much closer together than gas molecules in air. The flowing and bouncing of liquid molecules creates greater pressure than the pressure created by air.

The activity you are about to do is sometimes called a "magic trick" or "science trick." You can do it because of the difference in pressure that results from the fact that water is a liquid and air is a gas.

Materials:

pie pan or shallow baking dish

cold water

empty soda can

stove or hot plate

oven mitt or tongs

Procedure:

1.   Fill the pie pan or dish with 2.5 cm of cold water. Place it on the counter.

2.   Put a small amount of water in the empty can.

3.   Have an adult heat the soda can on the burner or on the hot plate. Let the water in the can boil vigorously for about a minute. Steam should come out of the can.

4.   Use tongs or an oven mitt to quickly turn the can upside down in the pie pan.

Let's see if you can figure out what happened. Answer these questions for some clues:

1. Which has greater pressure—gas molecules or liquid molecules?

    _____

2. Which takes up more space—gas molecules or liquid molecules?

    _____

3. When you heated the can, into what state of matter did the water change?

    _____

4. When you turned the can upside down in the water, could air get into the can?

    _____

5. When you placed the can in the cold water, it cooled. What state of matter did the water change into then?

    _____

Before you heat the can, it is filled with water and air. When you heat it, the water inside changes to hot water vapor or steam. The steam pushes air out of the can. When the can is upside down in water, air cannot get into the can. But, there is steam still inside the can.

Placing the can in water cools the steam to water. The water drops that form take up less space inside the can than the steam did. There is more room for air in the can now, so the air pressure inside the can drops. The pressure of the air outside the can is greater than the pressure inside the can. The air pushes on the can, causing the can to become crushed!

High Pressure

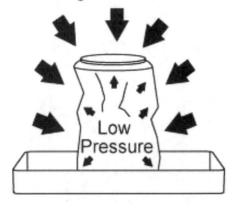

Name _____ Date _____

Pressure

Make a Barometer

A *barometer* is an instrument used to measure air pressure. It can help predict the weather. When air pressure drops, rainy weather may be on its way. Barometers often use mercury to measure air pressure. The mercury level rises in high pressure and falls in low pressure. When we use a barometer, we measure pressure in *millibars*, or millimeters of mercury.

You can make a simple barometer to observe air pressure. Try some tests with your barometer to see if you can use it to predict the weather.

Materials:

water

food coloring

empty soda bottle: about 500 mL (12 oz)

drinking straw

marker

ruler

eye dropper

clay

funnel

bowl

Procedure:

1. Use the marker to draw lines on the straw 1 cm apart.

2. In a bowl, mix a few drops of food coloring and some water. Then fill the soda bottle about 1/3 full of the colored water.

3. Hold the straw in the water until the bottom of the straw is just below the surface of the water.

4. Keep the straw in place by using clay to make an airtight seal at the top of the bottle.

5. With the eye dropper, fill the straw about half way with some colored water. Some of the water may gradually go from the straw into the bottle. However, if the water level in the straw does not remain at least a couple centimeters above the surface of the water in the bottle, then the seal around the straw is not tight enough or the bottom of the straw is not completely submerged in the water. In this case, remove the straw and clay and repeat steps 3 and 4, making sure the seal is airtight by using more clay.

6. Put the barometer outside in a place where the temperature will pretty much stay the same, such as in the shade.

7. On your chart, record what the weather is like outside. Then measure the height of the water in the straw, starting from the marks on the bottom, and record the measurement on your chart.

Continue observing your barometer for the next four days and recording the weather and your measurements.

Observations:

Record your data in the chart below.

Data	Day 01	Day 02	Day 03	Day 04	Day 05
Weather					
Height of Water					

Analysis:

1. What happened to the water in the drinking straw each day?

    _____

    _____

    _____

    _____

2. Was the water in the straw affected by the weather? How do you know?

    _____

    _____

    _____

    _____

3. If the air pressure outside the bottle changes, will the water inside the straw change?

_____

_____

_____

_____

Conclusions:

Write a paragraph explaining how you can observe air pressure using a barometer.

_____

_____

_____

_____

_____

_____

_____

_____

Student Guide

Optional: Balanced and Unbalanced Forces

Force is either a push or a pull. Forces are balanced if an object is not in motion. Forces are unbalanced if an object is in motion. This lesson will have you use what you know about forces and conduct an investigation to record evidence that an object has balanced or unbalanced forces.

Lesson Objectives

- Observe and/or take measurements of an object's motion to provide evidence that a pattern can be used to predict future motion.
- Plan and conduct an investigation to provide evidence of the effects of balanced and unbalanced forces on the motion of an object.

PREPARE

Approximate lesson time is 60 minutes.

Materials

For the Student

> Toy car
>
> String
>
> Unbalanced Forces Assignment

LEARN

Activity 1: Balanced and Unbalanced Forces *(Online)*

Instructions

Read about balanced and unbalanced forces. You will learn that objects in motion have unbalanced forces in the form of a push or a pull.

Activity 2: Forces in Action *(Online)*

Instructions

You will plan and conduct an investigation that utilizes a toy car and a string to demonstrate, measure, and observe push and pull forces. You will then complete the investigation assignment on unbalanced forces.

Activity 3: Lesson Review *(Online)*

ASSESS

Lesson Assessment: Optional: Balanced and Unbalanced Forces *(Online)*

You will complete an online assessment covering the main objectives of the lesson.

Name _____ . Date _____

Assignment
Unbalanced Forces

This investigation is to observe and record measurements on balanced and unbalanced forces.

Activity 1

1. Choose an object in your home that can move.

   _____

   _____

2. Find something that can be used to pull your movable object.

   _____

   _____

3. Find a way to measure and record motion.

   _____

   _____

4. Find a space to conduct your test.

   _____

   _____

5. Plan your test of push and pull forces on the object.

   _____

   _____

   _____

   _____

6. Record your measurements of distance traveled here.

_____

_____

7. Apply both a push and a pull force on the object at the same time and record the distance traveled.

_____

_____

8. What will happen to an object that has an unbalanced force?

_____

_____

_____

_____

9. Where will a shoe go if you have created an unbalanced force on it by pulling the shoelace toward you?

_____

_____

_____

_____

10. What was the distance that you pushed your object? Predict what would happen if you pushed your object again with the same amount of force three more times. What pattern would you expect? Why?

_____

_____

_____

_____

11. Imagine you pulled your object 20 centimeters from the starting point and stopped. If you pulled your object with less force, would you predict that the object would move more or less than 20 centimeters? Why?

_____

_____

_____

_____

Student Guide

Optional: Forces in Flight

Have you ever wondered how planes and birds are able to fly? Learn how air pressure and four important forces—lift, weight, thrust, and drag—play important roles in flight.

Lesson Objectives

- Describe the forces present in flight: lift, weight, thrust, and drag.
- Recognize that density of a solid stays the same even if the object's shape or size changes.

PREPARE

Approximate lesson time is 60 minutes.

Materials

For the Student

> How Does an Airplane Fly?
> household item - spatula
> plastic - container, lg, or bathtub
> paper clip (10)
> paper, notebook - 5 cm x 25 cm (2" x 10")
> scissors
> water
> paper, 8 1/2" x 11"

Keywords and Pronunciation

Daniel Bernoulli (DAHN-yuhl bur-NOOL-ee)

drag: The push that holds an object back as it moves through a gas or liquid. Drag is the opposite force created when the thrust of the engine causes the airplane to meet with air resistance.

lift: The upward force acting on an airfoil. Lift is the force that allows planes to take off and rise into the air.

thrust: A force or push. The engine of an airplane is what causes the force of thrust to occur.

weight: The result of the force of gravity acting on mass. Weight is measured in newtons.

LEARN

Activity 1: Optional: Lesson Instructions (*Online*)

This lesson is OPTIONAL. It is provided for students who seek enrichment or extra practice. You may skip this lesson.

If you choose to skip this lesson, then go to the Plan or Lesson Lists page and mark this lesson "Skipped" in order to proceed to the next lesson in the course.

Activity 2: Optional: The Forces Involved in Flight *(Online)*

Activity 3: Optional: How Does an Airplane Wing Work? *(Offline)*

Investigate how simple changes in air pressure can lift a 200-ton airplane high into the sky.

Safety

If you use a bathtub instead of a large container, do not leave your student unattended while the bathtub is full of water.

Activity 4: Optional: Paper Airplanes *(Online)*

Practice your fluid dynamics by designing and flying paper airplanes.

Safety

As usual, you may wish to preview any books or websites listed in this lesson.

Name _____   Date _____

Forces in Flight
How Does an Airplane Fly?

Airplanes can weigh nearly 200 tons, so how do they ever get off the ground? Keep in mind that:

- Rushing air hits the bottom of the wing and pushes it up while being deflected downward.
- Air also travels over the top of the wing. It follows the top surface smoothly all the way to the back of the wing, and the shape of the wing causes this air to move downward off the back of the wing.
- All this air pulled downward by the wing, causes the wing to be pulled upward.

You can demonstrate both ways that a wing is lifted up.

Materials

notebook paper, 5 cm x 25 cm (2 in x 10 in) strip

book

paper clips (10)

scissors

kitchen utensil – spatula

water

container, large, or bathtub

Demonstrate that rushing air hits the bottom of the wing and pushes it up.

1. Fill a bathtub or very large container with water.

2. Place a spatula underwater and tilt the flat part up a little, like an airplane wing.

3. Push the spatula through the water. You should be able to feel the spatula being pushed up by the water as you move it through.

Demonstrate that rushing air over the top of the wing sticks close to the wing.

1. Cut a strip of paper 5 cm x 25 cm. Hold one end against your chin, below your mouth.

2. Blow over the top of the strip. As the air tries to stay close to the paper, it pulls the paper up. The paper should rise.

3. Attach a paper clip to the end of the strip and repeat steps 2 and 3. Then add more paper clips to see how many you can lift this way.

Just as the air moving over the top of the wing helps keep a plane in the sky, blowing on the paper causes it to rise. The moving air near the top of the paper stays close to the paper, and so gets pulled down by the curved paper. This pulldown on the air (action) is balanced by a pull up on the paper (reaction)—the paper rises up.

1. What happens to the paper when you stop blowing?

_____

_____

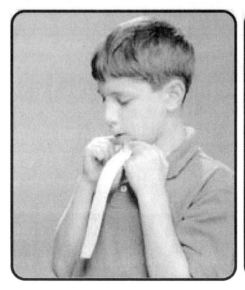 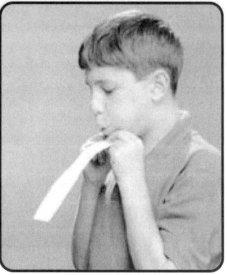

Review the information in the Explore activity. Label the picture of the airplane with the words *lift*, *thrust*, *drag*, and *weight*. Illustrate how the air pushes on the bottom and pulls on the top of the wing.

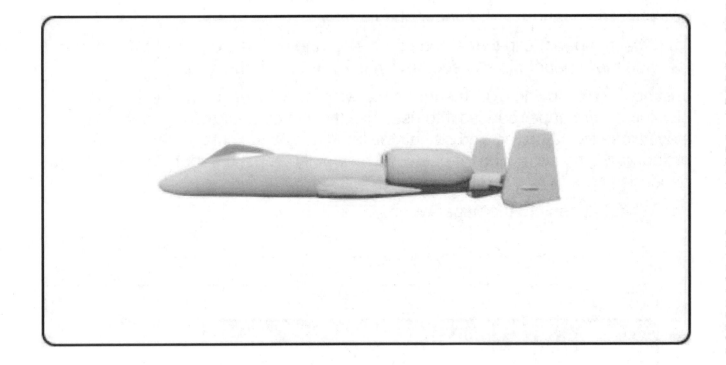

Student Guide

Optional: Density

You may have heard the word dense used to describe something thick or heavy, such as dense fog, or dense traffic. But you can use the word density to describe something as light as a gold coin or as heavy as a huge plastic foam ball. Density depends on what type of molecules an object is made of and how tightly packed they are. Find out how to calculate density, then find the density of materials on your own.

Lesson Objectives

- Define *density* as how tightly the matter of an object is packed together.
- Compare the densities of objects with the same shape and volume.
- Recognize that density of a solid stays the same even if the object's shape or size changes.
- Predict whether a substance will sink or float by comparing its density with the density of water.

PREPARE

Approximate lesson time is 60 minutes.

Materials

For the Student

> Air Density
> household item - tape measure
> balloon (2)
> bowl
> water - hot
> water - ice

Keywords and Pronunciation

density: The mass of an object divided by its volume. A baseball has a higher density than a plastic ball of the same size.

mass: The amount of stuff in any object. The mass of an object is the same on Earth as it is on the moon.

volume: The amount of space any object takes up. You can measure the volume of a liquid using a graduated cylinder.

LEARN

Activity 1: Optional: Lesson Instructions (*Online*)

This lesson is OPTIONAL. It is provided for students who seek enrichment or extra practice. You may skip this lesson.

If you choose to skip this lesson, then go to the Plan or Lesson Lists page and mark this lesson "Skipped" in order to proceed to the next lesson in the course.

Activity 2: Optional: Mass Divided by Volume (*Online*)

Activity 3: Optional: Density and Air Temperature (*Offline*)

Using balloons, explore how the density of air varies with changes in temperature.

Name _____ Date _____

Density

Air Density

Warm air and cold air have different densities. Molecules in cold temperatures move slower and are packed more tightly together. Molecules in warm temperatures move more quickly and take up lots of space. Now that you know some more about density, here is a way to demonstrate differences of the density of air.

1. Blow up a balloon and measure its circumference. (Wrap the tape measure all the way around.)
2. Put the balloon in hot water for 10 minutes.
3. Remove the balloon and measure its circumference.
4. Put the balloon in ice water for 10 minutes.
5. Remove the balloon and measure its circumference.

1. Did you notice a difference in the circumference of the balloons?

_____

_____

2. Why was the circumference of the balloon in hot water different than the one in ice water?

_____

_____

3. Knowing this, at which temperature did the balloon have more density? Hot or cold?

_____

_____

Student Guide

Optional: Buoyancy

Sinking and floating are directly related to an object's density. Buoyancy is the tendency of an object to float. An object will float if it is less dense than the substance it is in, such as water or air. Investigate the density and buoyancy of objects in different liquids and create a model submarine to explore a real-world example of how they are related.

Lesson Objectives

- Define buoyancy as an object's tendency to float.
- Explain Archimedes' observation that the buoyant force of water on an object is equal to the weight of water that the object displaces.
- Predict whether a substance will sink or float by comparing its density with the density of water.
- Recognize that an object denser than water will sink unless it is shaped so that the total density of the object is less than an equal volume of water.

PREPARE

Approximate lesson time is 60 minutes.

Materials

For the Student

> Liquid Layers
> cup, plastic (4)
> drinking glass - clear
> crayons, 64 colors or more - same 4 colors as food coloring
> food coloring - 4 colors
> funnel
> graduated cylinder
> markers - permanent
> oil, cooking
> rubbing alcohol
> spoon
> water
> Bottle Submarine
> bathtub
> clay
> tubing, plastic aquarium - 63.5 cm (25 inches)
> bottle, plastic - 500 mL (20 oz.)
> scissors
> tape, clear
> washer, metal - (2.5 cm/1 in diameter) (3)
> cup, plastic - clear
> dimes (10)
> golf ball

marbles
table-tennis ball
paper, 8 1/2" x 11"
tape, masking

Keywords and Pronunciation

Archimedes (ahr-kuh-MEE-deez)

Archimedes' Principle: Any body in a fluid is acted upon by a buoyant force equal to the weight of fluid displaced by the body.

buoyancy (BOY-uhnt-see): the tendency of an object to float

King Hieron (HIY-uh-rahn)

LEARN

Activity 1: Optional: Lesson Instructions (*Online*)

This lesson is OPTIONAL. It is provided for students who seek enrichment or extra practice. You may skip this lesson.

If you choose to skip this lesson, then go to the Plan or Lesson Lists page and mark this lesson "Skipped" in order to proceed to the next lesson in the course.

Activity 2: Optional: What Sinks, What Floats? (*Online*)

Activity 3: Optional: Liquid Layers (*Offline*)

A substance, whether solid or liquid, will not float in water if it is denser than the water. Learn about the densities of some liquid substances by trying to float them in water.

Activity 4: Optional: Bottle Submarine (*Offline*)

How do submarines manage to both sink underwater and rise to the surface?

Activity 5: Optional: The Physics of Underwater Diving (*Offline*)

For scuba divers to explore the deep regions of the ocean, they must wear a weight belt to help them sink. It is important for the weight belt to have just enough mass to sink the diver. But too much weight will to prevent the diver from coming back to the surface.

Investigate how much weight is needed to sink a very light diver.

1. Fill a plastic cup about 2/3 of the way with water. Mark the water level with a piece of masking tape.

2. Place a table-tennis ball in the cup of water. Observe the changes in the water level.

3. Push the table-tennis ball down so it is halfway submerged. Observe the water level.

4. Tape a dime to the ball and return it to the water. Does it float?

5. Continue taping dimes until the table-tennis ball sinks.

6. Try the same activity with a golf ball and marble. Try predicting first how many dimes you will need to sink them.

Divers want to have *neutral buoyancy,* which means they neither sink nor rise. Investigate how many dimes it takes to give the table-tennis ball neutral buoyancy.

Name _____ Date _____

Buoyancy

Liquid Layers

You've seen things floating all the time—leaves in a pond, helium balloons in midair, big rubber rafts in swimming pools—all of which are kept floating by something called a *buoyant force*. A buoyant force works like this:

- An object ends up in the water or the air.
- Gravity pulls the object toward Earth.
- Water or air pushes back on the object. (This pushing is buoyant force.)

In air or in water, what's the difference between an object that floats and an object that sinks? It has to do with density. If an object is denser than water or air, gravity will pull harder on it than water or air pushes up. The object will sink. If the object is less dense than water or air, the force of gravity will be overcome by the force of water or air pushing up.

Like solids, liquids have mass, volume, and density. Investigate the density of different liquids by finding out if they will sink or float in water.

Materials:

glass, clear drinking	honey
plastic cups (4)	water
marker, permanent	food coloring (blue)
spoon	graduated cylinder
rubbing alcohol	funnel
cooking oil	crayons

Procedure:

1. Use a marker to label the cups *water*, *honey*, *cooking oil*, and *rubbing alcohol.*

2. Pour 60 mL of water, honey, cooking oil, and rubbing alcohol into the proper cups.

3. Add one drop of food coloring to the alcohol and stir it with a spoon. This will help you tell the difference between the alcohol and the water.

4. One at a time, slowly pour each cup of liquid through the funnel and into the glass. Observe the glass for a few minutes to see what happens to the different liquids.

Observations:

1. What happens to the four different liquids when you mixed them together in the glass?

   _____

   _____

   _____

   _____

2. Use crayons the color of the food coloring to draw what the liquids look like in the glass.

3. This experiment deals with the density and buoyancy of substances. If a substance is denser than water, it will sink to the bottom. List the liquids you tested in order of density from least dense to densest.

   _____

   _____

   _____

   _____

Name _____   Date _____

Buoyancy
Bottle Submarine

Now you know how the buoyant force of water and of air keeps objects afloat. This time, you'll examine the density of the water and air themselves.

A submarine floats and sinks by taking in air and taking in water at different times. Which helps the submarine sink? Which helps it float? It's based on density. You know that water is denser than air, so when a submarine takes in water, it sinks.

Materials:

clay

tape

scissors

bathtub

500 mL (20 oz) plastic bottle

3 metal washers (2.5 c /1 inch in diameter)

63.5 cm (25 inches) of plastic aquarium tubing

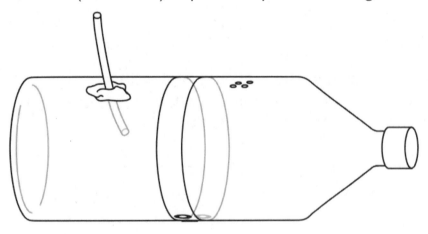

Procedure:

1. Use the scissors or another sharp object to punch four holes, about 0.5 cm in diameter, in the bottle. Place the holes 2 to 3 cm apart.

2. Tape three metal washers around the center of the bottle.

3. Punch another hole below the metal washers large enough to insert the plastic tubing.

4. Insert about 8 cm of the tubing into the hole in the bottle. Seal the opening with clay.

5. Place the submarine in the water. Record your observations below.

6. With the holes pointing upward, push the bottle down into the water. Record your observations.

7. Blow hard into the tubing of the submarine. Record what happens.

8. Repeat steps 5 to 7.

Observations:

1. When I first put the bottle in the water…

_____

_____

2. When I pushed the bottle down…

_____

_____

3. When I blew into the straw…

_____

_____

Analysis:

1. Why did the submarine float at first? Use the words such as *dense* or *density* and *buoyancy* or *buoyancy force*.

_____

_____

_____

_____

2. What happened to the submarine when you pushed it down that caused it to sink?

_____

_____

_____

_____

3. What happened when you blew air into the tubing?

_____

_____

_____

_____

4. How do you think submarines rise and sink in the water?

_____

_____

_____

_____

Student Guide

Optional: Shape and Buoyancy

Here's a situation that doesn't seem to make sense: a steel nail will sink to the bottom of a bucket of water, but a huge steel ocean liner floats easily on the ocean. What do you think? Confused? Luckily, science has a way of explaining. The answer has to deal with not just density, but overall density and how an object is shaped. Investigate shape and buoyancy and try to design an unsinkable clay boat.

Lesson Objectives

- Identify how the shape of an object affects its ability to float.
- Recognize that an object denser than water will sink unless it is shaped so that the total density of the object is less than an equal volume of water.
- Define pressure as the force exerted on a surface and recognize that pressure is measured in a unit called the pascal.

PREPARE

Approximate lesson time is 60 minutes.

Materials

For the Student

Unsinkable!
clay
bowl - large
graduated cylinder
spring scale
water

Keywords and Pronunciation

buoyancy (BOY-uhnt-see): the tendency of an object to float

LEARN

Activity 1: Optional: Lesson Instructions (*Online*)

This lesson is OPTIONAL. It is provided for students who seek enrichment or extra practice. You may skip this lesson.

If you choose to skip this lesson, then go to the Plan or Lesson Lists page and mark this lesson "Skipped" in order to proceed to the next lesson in the course.

Activity 2: Optional: How Does Shape Affect Buoyancy? (*Online*)

Activity 3: Optional: Unsinkable! (*Online*)

Ever wonder why a steel nail sinks but a steel ocean liner floats? Investigate how changing the shape of an object that is denser than water allows it to float.

Name _____   Date _____

Shape and Buoyancy
Unsinkable!

Remember, the difference in buoyancy between a sinking steel anchor and a floating steel boat is in the overall density of each. When an object goes in water, it displaces a certain amount. If it floats, you know that the weight of the water displaced equals the weight of the object below the water-line.

Because of its shape, the boat lets a lot of air between its sides. That means its overall density is less than the water it displaces, which means it has to float. Another way to say this is that the force of gravity pulling down on the boat and the buoyant force of the water pushing up are balanced.

If the boat suddenly displaces less water than its overall weight—say if it springs a leak, and all that air inside is replaced by water—down it goes. The force of gravity pulling on it will overcome the buoyant force of the water pushing up.

You can demonstrate this with water, plates and bowls, a spring scale, a graduated cylinder, and some clay. In this experiment you will measure mass in grams, which has an equivalent weight in newtons.

Materials:

modeling clay

spring scale

plate or large dish

bowl

graduated cylinder

Procedure:

1. Make a clay ball with a mass of 50 g. Use the gram side of the spring scale to measure mass.

2. Shape the clay into a boat that will float. Try making a flat circle, then folding over one of the edges, forming a very shallow cone.

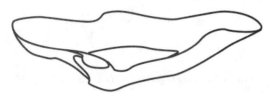

3. Test your boat in a bowl of water. Then empty the bowl.

4. Use the bowl to make sure your clay boat floats.

5. Once your boat floats, set the empty bowl in the dish. Fill the bowl with water to the very top. Be careful! Don't let any spill over the edge.

6. Carefully place your boat on the water's surface. Some water should spill over.

7. Remove the boat and very carefully remove the bowl from the dish.

8. Pour the water collected in the dish into the graduated cylinder.

Observations:

Before you complete your observations, there is something you should know. One milliliter of water has a mass of one gram. So for water, 1 g = 1 mL. If you had 20 mL of water, its mass would be 20 g.

1. Read the measurement on the graduated cylinder. How much water was displaced by the boat?

_____

2. What is the mass of the water displaced by the boat?

_____

3. Is the mass of the water displaced equal to the mass of the boat? (if not, see below)

_____

If the masses are not equal, they should be very close. This is most likely due to experimenter error, which happens in science. Look for clues that show a mistake may have been made. Is there a small amount of water still in the dish? Did you spill extra water into the dish when you moved the bowl? Did your clay have a mass of **EXACTLY** 50 g? You know how scientists must repeat tests. Try the activity again to see if you get any closer.

Conclusions:

1. For an object to float in water, how much water must that object displace?

   _____

   _____

2. Explain which forces are balanced when an object floats in water.

   _____

   _____

3. Explain how forces compare when an object sinks in water.

   _____

   _____

   _____

4. Imagine a great big pool toy in the shape of Godzilla. When Godzilla is deflated, he sinks. When he is blown up, he floats. Use the words "density" and "displace" to explain the differences between the sinking and the floating Godzilla.

   _____

   _____

   _____

Student Guide

Optional: Forces in Fluids: Unit Review

Learning about science answers many questions you have about the world. After handling the "pressure" of this unit, you can now describe many things about Forces in Fluids. You know about the forces in flight and why a boat floats. You can also figure out if a buried treasure actually contains hundreds of kilograms of gold. Review these concepts, and then take the unit assessment.

Lesson Objectives

- Define pressure as the force exerted on a surface and recognize that pressure is measured in a unit called the pascal.
- Describe the forces present in flight: lift, weight, thrust, and drag.
- Explain that atmospheric pressure decreases with height above sea level and water pressure increases with depth below sea level.
- Measure the density of a substance or object and predict whether it will sink or float in water.
- Recognize that an object denser than water will sink unless it is shaped so that the total density of the object is less than an equal volume of water.

PREPARE

Approximate lesson time is 60 minutes.

LEARN

Activity 1: Optional: Lesson Instructions (*Online*)

This lesson is OPTIONAL. It is provided for students who seek enrichment or extra practice. You may skip this lesson.

If you choose to skip this lesson, then go to the Plan or Lesson Lists page and mark this lesson "Skipped" in order to proceed to the next lesson in the course.

Activity 2: Optional: Forces Review (*Online*)

Activity 3: Optional: Aerodynamic Olympics (*Online*)

After a successful Forces in Fluids unit, you are invited to show your knowledge at the Aerodynamic Olympics. These Olympics are a competition held between you and your computer. Answer correctly to win a gold, silver, or bronze medal at the end.

Activity 4: Optional: ZlugQuest Measurement (*Online*)

Student Guide

What's Weather?

- Identify forms of precipitation (rain, snow, sleet, and hail) and explain how they form.
- Use appropriate tools to measure and record weather conditions, including air temperature, wind direction, wind speed, humidity, and pressure.
- Explain that air masses meet at fronts and that most changes in the weather occur along fronts.
- Explain how air moves in cold and warm fronts, and identify the common weather patterns associated with each.
- Define *humidity* as the amount of water vapor in the air.
- Identify common weather patterns associated with changes in air pressure.
- Recognize that weather forecasters rely on data collected from various resources, such as weather stations, weather balloons, weather satellites, and weather radar.
- Interpret weather maps and their symbols, including those for precipitation, pressure, and fronts.

You can measure the weather, just like a meteorologist! Use two of the tools of a meteorologist, the thermometer and the Beaufort Wind Scale, to determine weather conditions.

Lesson Objectives

- Identify the four basic types of clouds: cumulus, cirrus, cumulonimbus, and stratus.
- Determine wind speed by using the Beaufort Wind Scale.
- Identify the kinds of precipitation (rain, snow, sleet, and hail) and explain how they form.
- Name two ways to determine wind direction.
- Use a thermometer to measure temperature.
- Explore concepts to be addressed during the year in Science 3.

PREPARE

Approximate lesson time is 60 minutes.

Advance Preparation

- It's important that you read the Course Introduction for Science 3 before your student begins the course. You can find the course introduction at the beginning of the What's Weather lesson.
- Throughout this unit, your student will be recording weather observations in a Science Notebook. Before you begin the first lesson, you may wish to help your student set up the notebook and a weather chart.
- Science Notebook
- Partly fill a 3-ring binder with ruled notebook paper. Use dividers to separate the notebook into 11 sections, one for each grade 3 Science unit.
- Weather Chart

1. Fold a piece of loose-leaf paper in half lengthwise, and then in half again so you have four columns when you open the paper.

2. Use a ruler to trace over the fold lines.

3. Record today's date in the upper left-hand column.

4. Label the remaining columns *1, 2,* and *3*. Add the time of each observation.

5. Add these labels below the date, skipping three lines between each label: *Temperature, Precipitation, Clouds, Wind Speed, Wind Direction.* You may use the following abbreviations: T, P, C, WS, and WD.

6. Draw a line under the record for the day and begin the next day's observations on the line below it. This will allow for multiple observations on a single side. Be sure to date each record.

Wind Forces

- In this lesson your student will have the opportunity to measure wind forces using a kite and a spring scale. If you plan to do this optional activity, you will need to use a spring scale that measures force in 5-newton increments. If you do not already have this type of spring scale, you will need to purchase one. Carolina Math and Science, as well as many other science supply companies, has color-coded spring scales.

Materials

For the Student

Making a Beaufort Spinner
brads
markers
paper, 8 1/2" x 11" - or larger
plate, paper (2)
ribbon - any color, 30cm (12 in)
ruler
scissors

Keywords and Pronunciation

Anders Celsius (SEL-see-uhs)

anemometer (a-nuh-MAH-muh-tur)**:** A tool used to measure the speed of the wind. Meteorologists use an anemometer to measure wind speed.

cirrus (SIHR-uhs)

contract: To take up less space, or to become smaller in volume. As the temperature decreases, the liquid in a thermometer contracts and moves down the tube.

cumulonimbus (kyoo-myuh-luh-NIM-buhs)

cumulus (KYOO-myuh-luhs)

evaporate: To change from a liquid to a gas. Water evaporates when it boils.

expand: To take up more space, or to increase in volume. As the temperature increases, the liquid in a thermometer expands and moves up the tube.

Francis Beaufort (BOH-furt)

Gabriel Fahrenheit (FAIR-uhn-hiyt)

mercury: A poisonous silver metal that stays liquid throughout a wide range of temperatures. Although mercury thermometers are more accurate than alcohol thermometers, for safety reasons, always use an alcohol thermometer.

meteorologist (mee-tee-uh-RAH-luh-jist): A person who studies the weather. A meteorologist uses tools to collect information about the weather.

precipitation: Water that falls from clouds as rain, hail, snow, or sleet. A weather map shows areas that are receiving precipitation.

water vapor: Water in the form of a gas. Water vapor forms when liquid water evaporates.

weather vane: A tool that shows the direction the wind is coming from. The weather vane on the roof showed that the wind was coming from the north.

LEARN

Activity 1: Welcome to Science 3 *(Online)*

Activity 2: Weather Measures Up *(Online)*

Learn about some of the tools meteorologists use to make weather observations. Identify the four main types of clouds, and find out how rain, snow, sleet, and hail form. Become familiar with the Beaufort Wind Scale.

Safety

Preview any recommended websites before having your student view them.

Activity 3: Make a Beaufort Spinner *(Offline)*

Activity 4: Weather Records *(Offline)*

Instructions

Meteorologists keep records to help them notice patterns in the weather, such as temperature, precipitation, cloud type, wind speed, and wind direction. You are going to collect weather information using tools that include a thermometer, a compass, and the Beaufort Wind Scale.

In your Science Notebook, set up a chart that will help you record the weather. You will be recording your observations three times a day during the next few weeks, and then looking at your data to see any weather patterns.

Collect your data every day, even on days that you do not have a Science lesson. Make your observations at the same three times each day: morning, midday, and evening. Each time you make observations, try to include all the following measurements: temperature, precipitation, cloud type, wind speed, and wind direction. If it is too dark to make your evening observations, record temperature and precipitation only.

Set Up Your Weather Chart

1. Fold a piece of loose-leaf paper in half lengthwise, and then in half again, so you have four columns when you open the paper.

2. Use a ruler to trace over the fold lines.

3. Record today's date in the upper left-hand column.

4. Label the remaining columns 1, 2, and 3 for your three daily measurements. Write the time of each observation.

5. Add these labels below the date, skipping three lines between each label: Temperature, Precipitation, Clouds, Wind Speed, Wind Direction. You may wish to use the following abbreviations: T, P, C, WS, and WD.

6. Use the backside of the paper to record the next day's observations. Remember to write the date and times each day.

Weather Observations

Record the following observations on your chart. Keep the chart in your Science Notebook. Air Temperature

1. Place the thermometer in a shady location, out of direct sunlight and off the ground, for approximately 10 minutes before you make a reading.

2. Predict the temperature of the air before you take your measurement. With practice, you will be able to make a rough estimate of air temperature just by being outside.

3. Measure the temperature first in degrees Celsius and then in degrees Fahrenheit. Keep your eyes level with the thermometer. Use the symbols °C and °F to record the temperature on your chart.

Precipitation

Record the type of precipitation: rain, snow, sleet, hail. If there is no precipitation, indicate that on your chart as well.

Clouds

If possible, identify and record the types of clouds. You may see more than one type of cloud in the sky at the same time. If you are not able to identify the types, make a quick sketch of the clouds on your chart.

Wind Speed and Direction

Use your Beaufort spinner and ribbon to determine wind speed. Write the description on the chart. Use the compass to determine wind direction.

1. Hold the compass flat on your palm with the North label at the top.

2. Turn so the compass needle lines up with the North label. You are now facing north. For future observations, remember which direction is north. Locate south, east, and west.

3. Hold up your ribbon again to see which way it blows. Because wind direction is named for the direction from which the wind is blowing, record the direction opposite the ribbon's tail. For example, if the tail blows to the east, record the wind direction as west, because the wind is coming from the west. You may use the following symbols to record wind direction on your chart: N, NE, E, SE, S, SW, W, NW.

Repeat these measurements at three different times during the day, then at the same times each following day, being sure to record the times you take the measurements.

At the end of each day, circle the lowest temperature in blue and highest temperature in red.

ASSESS

Lesson Assessment: What's Weather? *(Offline)*

Sit with an adult to review the assessment questions.

LEARN

Activity 5: Optional: Wind Forces *(Offline)*

Wind Forces

You might have noticed that the wind seems to blow differently near the ground than at the tops of trees. The wind at the tops of tall trees might be much stronger or weaker than the wind near the ground. You can find out how the wind changes with height by measuring wind force using a kite and a spring scale. A *force* is nothing more than a push or a pull. When a kite lifts into the air, the amount of pull you feel tugging on the string is related to the strength of the wind pushing the kite in the opposite direction.

A *spring scale* is an instrument that measures force—the strength of the push or pull. A spring scale measures force in units called *newtons*, named after the famous scientist, Sir Isaac Newton. The symbol for a newton is N.

Investigate

1. Tie a string approximately 6 meters long to your kite.
2. At every meter along the string, tie a small loop so you can hook the spring scale onto the loops.
3. Secure the spring scale to the very end of the string.
4. Allow the wind to lift the kite as high as it can go. Hold the spring scale in your hand and measure the force of the wind.
5. Pull in the string meter by meter, hooking the spring scale in each loop and reading the force.

Conclude

Was the force of the wind the same at each height?

At which height was the wind the strongest? The weakest?

In your first measurement you used a string that was 6 meters long, but were you measuring the force of the wind exactly 6 meters high? [1] Why or why not? [2]

Name _____   Date _____

What's Weather?

Making a Beaufort Spinner

1. Look at the Beaufort scale on the last screen of the Explore.

2. Trace around a paper plate on a sheet of paper. With that sheet of paper, cut out the circle and divide it with a marker into six equal parts.

3. Cut out the inner circle from one plate, then cut out a V-shape that matches one of the six segments of the paper circle. Note: end the cuts before you reach the very center of the circle.

4. For your spinner, you will use the numbers 0,2,4,6,8, and 11 from the Beaufort scale in the Explore Activity. For each section of the spinner, write the number, write the brief description, and draw the flag as it is shown for that number in the Explore activity diagram.

5. Turn a paper plate upside down. Use a brad (labeled below) to attach the large and small circles to the center of the plate as shown.

Use your Beaufort spinner to decide how hard the wind is blowing right now. Step outside and hold up a piece of ribbon and note how it blows in the wind. Then take a look at your Beaufort spinner. Compare the pictures on your spinner to the way the ribbon is moving. The Beaufort scale will help you decide how fast the wind is blowing. Notice that the pictures on your spinner tell you the number on the Beaufort scale that matches the description of the wind speed. Which number on the scale describes how hard the wind is blowing right now?

Student Guide
Charting Weather

Weather is always talked about because it is always changing. In North America, we expect December, January, and February to bring lower temperatures because these months are in winter. People record and graph weather data to see patterns and make predictions about future weather.

Lesson Objectives

- Represent data in tables or graphical displays to describe typical weather conditions expected during a particular season.

PREPARE

Approximate lesson time is 60 minutes.

Materials

For the Student

Weather Graphs and Charts Assignment

LEARN

Activity 1: Weather Tools *(Online)*

Instructions

Read about different tools used to record and predict weather.

Activity 2: Charting Weather *(Online)*

Instructions

Interpret and add to graphs and charts using weather data in the Weather Graphs and Charts Assignment.

ASSESS

Lesson Assessment: Charting Weather *(Online)*

Sit with an adult to review the assessment questions.

Name _____   Date _____

Assignment

Weather Graphs and Charts

This investigation is to record weather measurements in graphs and charts. Use the data provided for you and answer questions and complete the graphs on temperature and rainfall.

1. The bar graph shows the average rainfall for the summer months in Florida. August does not have data. Record on the graph that August had 9 inches of rain.

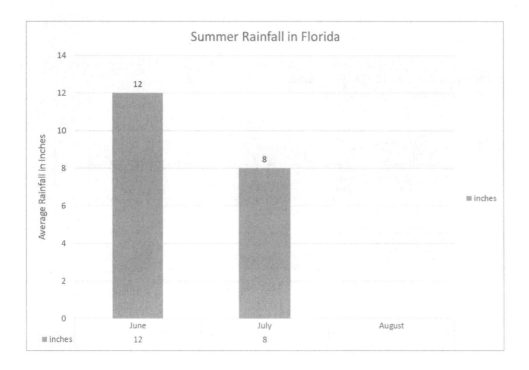

2. In winter, Michigan can get very cold. Look at the data table and complete the line graph with the temperatures in the table.

Month	Temperature in Fahrenheit
December	22 degrees
January	17 degrees
February	19 degrees

Answer:

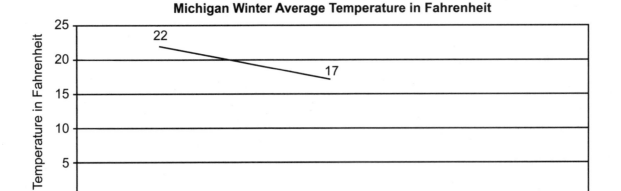

Michigan Winter Average Temperature in Fahrenheit

3. Now, create a graph to show the average rainfall for each month shown in the data table for the state of Louisiana in the spring.

Month	Rainfall in Inches
March	5.5
April	5
May	4.5

Answer:

4. Look at the graph you made for question 3. What weather would you expect for June based on the pattern from your graph?

_____

_____

_____

_____

Student Guide
Weather Fronts

How does the weather change from day to day? Why does the wind blow? Air masses that meet at fronts are the key to changes in wind and weather.

Lesson Objectives

- Define *humidity* as the amount of water vapor in the air.
- Explain how air moves in cold and warm fronts.
- Explain that air masses meet at fronts, and that most changes in the weather occur along fronts.

PREPARE

Approximate lesson time is 60 minutes.

Advance Preparation

- Assemble a science notebook if you have not already done so. Your student will use the notebook throughout the year to record observations.

Keywords and Pronunciation

cirrus (SIHR-uhs)

humidity: The amount of water vapor in the air. When the papers on my desk curled up, I knew there was a lot of humidity in the room.

humidity: The amount of water vapour in the air. When the papers on my desk curled up, I knew there was a lot of humidity in the room.

hygrometer (hiy-GRAH-muh-tuhr): A tool used to measure the humidity in the air. The reading on the hygrometer told the meteorologist that the air was less humid today than yesterday.

meteorologist (mee-tee-uh-RAH-luh-jist): A person who studies the weather. A meteorologist uses tools to collect information about the weather.

Safety

Be careful when using straight pins.

Never look directly into the sun.

LEARN

Activity 1: Fronts Bring Changes (Online)

Activity 2: How Humid Is It? (Offline)

Instructions

In this activity, you will build a simple tool to measure humidity. The tool uses a scale made of construction paper and a pointer made from a straw balanced on a pivot. When the humidity of the air changes, the pointer will turn on the pivot and move up or down the scale to reflect the change in humidity.

1. Create the Indicator

Cut out five construction-paper squares 5 cm x 5 cm. Punch a hole in the center of each square, and thread all the squares onto the drinking straw. The squares should be approximately 1/2 cm apart on the straw. Use a piece of clay to fasten the toothpick to one end of the straw. The toothpick will serve as the pointer for the humidity tester.

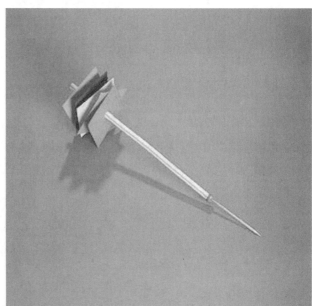

2. Make the Scale

On a piece of construction paper, draw a triangle that is 15 cm tall and 10 cm wide.

Cut out the triangle, and then fold it in half lengthwise.

Draw lines at 1/2 cm intervals up the fold.

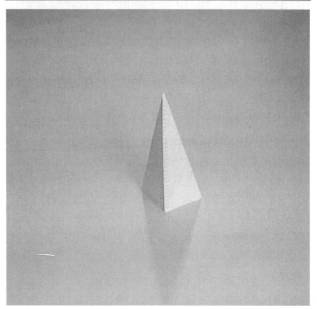

3. Make the Pivot

Cut another piece of construction paper, 15 cm x 5 cm, to serve as the pivot for the pointer. Fold the pivot as shown in the photo. Cut a small V-shaped notch across both top edges. The notches will serve as the balance for the pointer.

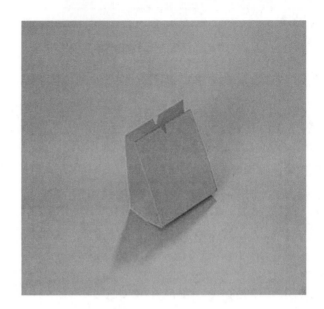

4. Glue the Pivot

Glue the base of the pivot and the triangular scale to the lid of the shoebox.

5. Tape the Pivot

Tape one side of the paper pivot together as shown.

6. Balance the Indicator

Stick a pin through the straw, then balance the pin across the notches in the pivot. The straw must balance on the pivot with the pin. Adjust this by adding or removing clay from the pointer end. The squares of paper may also be moved up and down the straw to help balance this part. You may also adjust the placement of the pin within the straw.

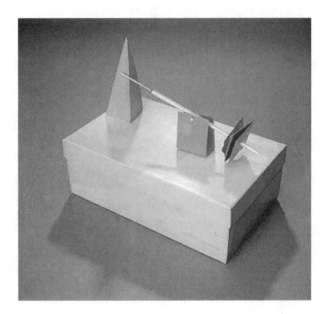

Note the position of the pointer. As the air becomes more humid (gathers more water vapor) the paper squares at the end of the pointer will absorb some of the water. As the paper collects moisture, it becomes heavier and pulls down the end of the pointer opposite the scale.

To read your humidity tester, count the notches from the bottom of the scale to the level of the toothpick. Record this number as the humidity of the air.

Safety

Be careful when using straight pins.

Activity 3: Weather Records *(Offline)*

Which types of clouds do you see in the sky right now?

In your Science Notebook, continue to record the following information: temperature, precipitation, clouds, wind speed, wind direction, and humidity.

Repeat these measurements three times each day, morning, midday, and evening. Be sure to record the time you took the measurements. At the end of each day, circle the lowest temperature in blue and highest temperature in red.

As you record your measurements, begin to compare your observations.

Safety

Never look directly into the sun.

ASSESS

Lesson Assessment: Weather Fronts *(Offline)*

Sit with an adult to review the assessment questions.

LEARN

Activity 4: Optional: Create Dew *(Offline)*

Have you ever walked outside barefooted in the grass in the morning? Did your feet get wet? If it didn't rain the night before, that dampness could be morning dew. How did the dew get there? Look in your own yard for the answer!

1. **Dig**

Dig a hole in the ground approximately 1 foot deep and 5 inches wide. Put the plastic cup in the hole.

2. **Cover**

Cover the hole more than halfway with the plastic sheet and position the cup in the hole so it is directly under the edge of the plastic. Anchor the plastic in place with some heavy rocks, then place several small stones on the edge of the plastic sheet near the cup, so that the sheet slopes toward the cup.

3. **Observe**

Visit the site the next morning. What do you observe?

Cool air holds less water vapor than warm air. As the temperature falls at night, water vapor in the air condenses on the plastic sheet and drips into the cup. This is the same way dew forms on the grass in the morning. Something similar happens when you fill a glass with water and ice. The water vapor in the air condenses on the cool, outside surface of the glass.

Activity 5: Optional: ZlugQuest Measurement *(Online)*

Student Guide

Air Pressure

How does air pressure influence the weather? Learn how meteorologists observe patterns in air pressure to help them make forecasts.

Lesson Objectives

- Explain that a *barometer* is used to measure air pressure.
- State that high air pressure usually brings dry, sunny weather.
- State that low air pressure usually brings some type of precipitation.
- State that *wind* is air moving from areas of high pressure to areas of low pressure.

PREPARE

Approximate lesson time is 60 minutes.

Keywords and Pronunciation

air pressure: The amount of air pressing on a given surface area. Air pressure helps forecasters know what kind of weather to expect.

barometer (buh-RAH-muh-tuhr): A tool used to measure the pressure of the air. The barometer is rising, so I predict the weather will become sunny and dry.

Buys Ballot (bouees bah-LAWT)

meteorologist (mee-tee-uh-RAH-luh-jist): A person who studies the weather. A meteorologist uses tools to collect information about the weather.

LEARN

Activity 1: Under Pressure *(Online)*

Activity 2: Make a Barometer *(Offline)*

Instructions

1. Cut

Cut off the neck of the balloon.

2. Fasten

Stretch the balloon over the mouth of the jar and fasten it there with tape.

3. Tape

Tape two straws together.

4. Cut

Cut a small triangle from construction paper and attach it to the end of the straw as a pointer.

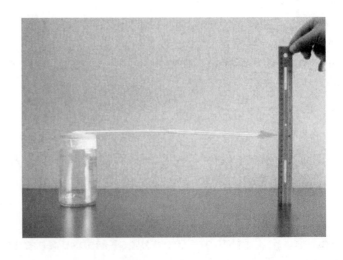

---

5. Tape

Tape the other end of the straw to the center of the balloon.

6. Check

Hold a ruler next to the pointer. Check the position of the pointer.

Check the reading every few hours. What do you notice? If the pointer moves up between readings, then the air pressure is rising, or increasing. When the pointer moves down, then the air pressure is falling, or decreasing. The change, up or down, in air pressure will help you predict the changes in weather that are coming.

When you record air pressure in your Science Notebook, use the ruler as the scale. Make sure you position your ruler the same way each time.

Activity 3: Weather Records *(Online)*

Continue recording the following information in your Science Notebook: temperature, precipitation, clouds, wind speed, wind direction, humidity and air pressure.

Repeat these measurements at three different times during the day, being sure to record the time you took the measurements. At the end of each day, circle the lowest temperature in blue and highest temperature in red. As you record your measurements continue to compare your observations. Do you see any patterns?

ASSESS

Lesson Assessment: Air Pressure *(Offline)*

Sit with an adult to review the assessment questions.

LEARN

Activity 4: Optional: ZlugQuest Measurement *(Online)*

Student Guide

Weather Forecasting

What do the symbols on a weather map represent? Learn how to look at a weather map and its symbols to help you predict the weather in your area.

Lesson Objectives

- Interpret weather maps and their symbols, including those for cloud cover, precipitation, temperature, pressure, and fronts.
- Recognize that weather forecasters rely on data collected from various sources, such as weather stations, weather balloons, weather satellites, and weather radar.

PREPARE

Approximate lesson time is 60 minutes.

Materials

For the Student

    Weather Map

Keywords and Pronunciation

forecast: A prediction of the weather based on readings from weather instruments. The forecast for today calls for snow.

hygrometer (hiy-GRAH-muh-tuhr)**:** A tool used to measure the humidity in the air. The reading on the hygrometer told the meteorologist that the air was less humid today than yesterday.

meteorologist (mee-tee-uh-RAH-luh-jist)**:** A person who studies the weather. A meteorologist uses tools to collect information about the weather.

weather station: A place where instruments gather information about the weather. We made a weather station that included a weathervane, anemometer, barometer, and thermometer.

LEARN

Activity 1: Mapping the Forecast *(Online)*

What do weather maps tell us? Explore their uses and how they help meteorologists predict and describe the weather.

Activity 2: Read a Weather Map *(Offline)*

Weather maps give information about the weather. Meteorologists use symbols to show a lot of information without using a lot of words. When a meteorologist looks at a weather map, he or she needs to know where it's raining, what type of clouds are in the area, where the cold and warm air is located, and where the air is moving. Use the weather map to guide your student through the activity below.

Look at the key on the weather map. Notice the symbols and what they stand for. Color the cold fronts blue and the warm fronts red.

Find California on the weather map. What symbols do you notice in that area? [1] The three lines stand for *fog*.

Also in California you will see one place where it is raining. A cold front is also moving through from the west. What does the weather feel like in a place that is experiencing a cold front? [2]

In what state do you see a thunderstorm? [3] What type of front is causing this thunderstorm? [4] Where is it snowing? [5]

Find North Dakota on your map. Is the air pressure in North Dakota high or low? [6] What might the weather be like there—dry and sunny or cloudy and rainy? [7]

Find the state where a warm front is bringing rain and fog. [8]

Find the place you live or choose a state. What's the weather like there? How do you know? [9]

Activity 3: Weather Records *(Offline)*

In your Science Notebook, continue recording the following information at three different times during the day: temperature, precipitation, clouds, wind speed, wind direction, humidity, and air pressure.

Repeat these measurements at three different times during the day, being sure to record the time you took the measurements. At the end of the day, circle the lowest temperature in blue and highest temperature in red.

Activity 4: Patterns in Weather Data *(Offline)*

ASSESS

Lesson Assessment: Weather Forecasting *(Online)*

You will complete an online assessment covering the main objectives of the lesson.

LEARN

Activity 5: Track the Weather *(Offline)*

Find a weather map of the United States in a newspaper or online.

Pick a state where a friend or relative lives. Keep track of the weather in their area for a week. You may choose to find the daily temperature, cloud cover, precipitation, and the fronts passing through their area. After observing the patterns for a week, try forecasting the next week's weather.

At the end of the week, call or write the friend or relative to share with them what you noticed about their weather, and give them your forecast. Contact them again to check your forecast. Was your forecast correct?

Student help

If you decide to look online, you can find a variety of maps on The Weather Channel site or the USA Today Weather page.

Activity 6: Weather Safety *(Online)*

Name _____   Date _____

Weather Forecasting
Weather Map

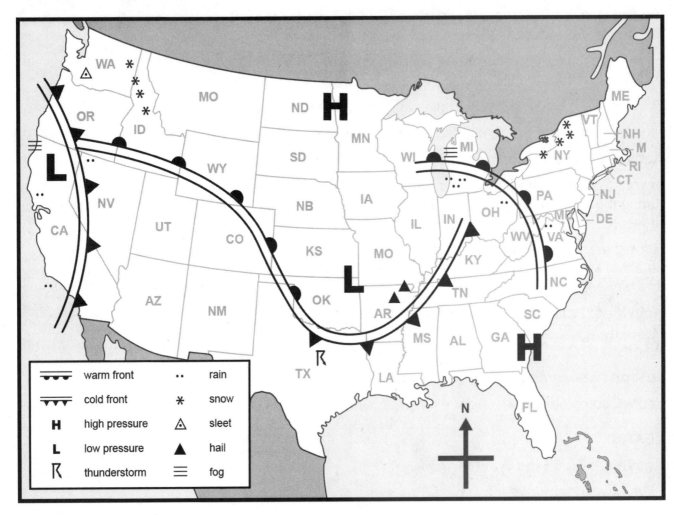

〰 warm front		••	rain
⌄⌄⌄ cold front		✳	snow
H high pressure		△	sleet
L low pressure		▲	hail
�R thunderstorm		☰	fog

Student Guide
Weather Safety

Weather can be pleasant or dangerous. You may have heard of tornados, lightning, or flooding. These things are called weather hazards because they can cause harm or damage. There are designs that have been created in order to keep people safe.

Lesson Objectives

- Make a claim about the merit of a design solution that reduces the impacts of a weather-related hazard.

PREPARE

Approximate lesson time is 60 minutes.

Materials

For the Student

　　Make a Claim Assignment

Keywords and Pronunciation

hypothermia: A sudden and dangerous drop in body temperature

frostbite: A condition in which body tissues freeze

hazard: A source of danger that can cause injury

claim: A statement that says what you believe

merit: Reasons why a claim is correct

LEARN

Activity 1: Weather Hazards *(Online)*

Activity 2: Lightning Design Solution *(Online)*

Activity 3: Lesson Review *(Online)*

ASSESS

Lesson Assessment: Weather Safety *(Offline)*

Sit with an adult to review the assessment questions.

Name_____   Date_____

Assignment
Make a Claim

This investigation is to make a claim based on the merit of a design solution. The weather hazard of flooding has many design solutions. Choose one design solution to focus on. Your options are between reservoirs or dams. Do some online research and support the merit of your chosen design solution.

1. Which design solution—reservoirs or dams—have you selected?

    _____

    _____

    _____

    _____

2. What is your claim, based on the merit of the design solution?

    _____

    _____

    _____

    _____

3. What is the merit of your claim, based on research?

    _____

    _____

    _____

    _____

Student Guide

Weather: Unit Review and Assessment

What have you learned about the weather? To prepare for the Unit Assessment, play a game and review what you've learned.

Lesson Objectives

- Define *humidity* as the amount of water vapor in the air.
- Explain that air masses meet at fronts and that most changes in the weather occur along fronts.
- Explain how air moves in cold and warm fronts and identify the common weather patterns associated with each.
- Identify common weather patterns associated with changes in air pressure.
- Identify the kinds of precipitation (rain, snow, sleet, and hail) and explain how they form.
- Interpret weather maps and their symbols, including those for precipitation, pressure, and fronts.
- Recognize that weather forecasters rely on data collected from various sources, such as weather stations, weather balloons, weather satellites, and weather radar.
- Use appropriate tools to measure and record weather conditions, including air temperature, wind direction, wind speed, humidity, and pressure.
- Explain how air moves in cold and warm fronts.
- Explain that air masses meet at fronts, and that most changes in the weather occur along fronts.
- Interpret weather maps and their symbols, including those for cloud cover, precipitation, temperature, pressure, and fronts.
- Determine wind speed by using the Beaufort Wind Scale.
- Explain that a *barometer* is used to measure air pressure.
- Name two ways to determine wind direction.
- Recognize that weather forecasters rely on data collected from various sources, such as weather stations, weather balloons, weather satellites, and weather radar.
- State that low air pressure usually brings some type of precipitation.
- Use a thermometer to measure temperature.

PREPARE

Approximate lesson time is 60 minutes.

Materials

For the Student

  What's the Weather? Game

Keywords and Pronunciation

meteorologist (mee-tee-uh-RAH-luh-jist)**:** A person who studies the weather. A meteorologist uses tools to collect information about the weather.

LEARN

Activity 1: Weather Unit *(Offline)*

What have you learned about the weather? To prepare for the Unit Assessment, play a game and review what you've learned.

Object

The object of the game is to collect one of each token: thermometer, cumulus cloud, snowflake, weathervane, and barometer. When you have collected one of each token, the forecast looks sunny!

Setup

Cut out the tokens and question cards. Shuffle the question cards and place them face down on the table. Use coins (or other small objects) for game-board pieces. Place them on "Start."

How to Play

1. Move forward one space at the beginning of each turn. Listen as the other player reads one question.

   - If you do not answer the question correctly, your turn is over. Move to a new space at the beginning of your next turn.
   - If you answer the question correctly, collect a token that matches the space on which you have landed.
   - If you answer a question while on the "Start" space, you can choose the token you want to collect.

2. Place each token you collect in one of your empty token squares on the game board. Move to a new space at the beginning of your next turn.

   - Collect only one of each type of token. A correct answer for a token you have already earned allows you to advance one space and answer a new question.

3. Take turns reading the questions and moving around the board. The game is over when one player collects one of each token. If the game ends before you have answered all of the questions, continue playing the game or read the questions aloud for review.

ASSESS

Unit Assessment: Weather *(Offline)*

Complete an offline Unit Assessment. Your learning coach will score the assessment.

LEARN

Activity 2: Optional: ZlugQuest Measurement *(Online)*

Name _____   Date _____

Weather: Unit Review and Assessment
What's the Weather? Game

Object

The object of the game is to collect one of each token: thermometer, cumulus cloud, snowflake, weathervane, and barometer. When you have collected one of each token the forecast looks sunny!

Setup

Cut out the tokens and question cards. Shuffle the question cards and place them face down on the table. Use coins (or other small objects) for game-board pieces. Place them on "Start."

How to Play

Move forward one space at the beginning of each turn. Listen as the other player reads one question. If you do not answer the question correctly, your turn is over. Move to a new space at the beginning of your next turn.

If you answer the question correctly, collect a token that matches the space on which you have landed. If you answer a question while on the "Start" space, you can choose which token you want to collect. Place the token in one of your empty token squares on the game board.

Move to a new space at the beginning of your next turn. Collect only one of each type of token. A correct answer for a token you have already earned allows you to advance one space and answer a new question. Take turns reading the questions and moving around the board. The game is over when one player collects one of each token. If the game ends before all of the question cards have been read, continue playing the game, or read the questions aloud for review.

cut

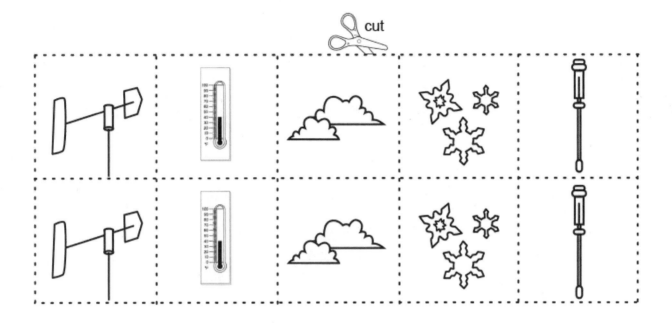

Cut out the question cards.

Q: What is a thermometer used to measure? A: air temperature	Q: What is a barometer used to measure? A: air pressure
Q: What does a weathervane measure? A: wind direction	Q: A hygrometer measures _____. A: humidity
Q: Wind speed is measured by an _____. A: anemometer	Q: How does sleet form? A: Raindrops freeze on their way down to Earth.
Q: Areas of low pressure on a weather map are shown using what symbol? A: L	Q: Name the four types of precipitation. A: sleet, snow, rain, hail

Q: Air masses meet at _____. A: fronts	Q: When you see this symbol ** on a weather map, what does it mean? A: It's snowing in that place.
Q: How do weather balloons help meteorologists forecast the weather? A: They collect data for meteorologists, such as temperature, wind direction and speed, air pressure, and humidity, at different heights above the ground.	Q: Precipitation generally occurs in areas of high or low air pressure? A: low
Q: Describe one way to determine wind direction. A: compass and ribbon; weathervane; by watching tree branches; by watching smoke from chimneys; by tossing grass clipping and watching them fall	Q: Wind is moving air flowing from areas of _____ pressure to areas of _____ pressure. A: high to low
Q: The amount of water vapor in the air is _____. A: humidity	Q: A dry, sunny day with clear skies usually means the air pressure is high or low? A: high

Q: From where do weather satellites take pictures of clouds? A: space or orbiting Earth	Q: Most changes in weather occur at fronts. Which of these is a symbol for a warm front? A:
Q: Name the type of front. Cold air quickly pushes under warm air causing strong winds and thunderstorms. A: cold front	Q: Name the type of front. Warm, moist air creeps slowly up over cold air bringing light winds, low stratus clouds, and rain or snow. A: warm front
Q: Name the type of precipitation: Winds move frozen water drops up and down inside clouds forming layers of ice that eventually fall to the ground. A: hail	Q: Name the type of precipitation: Tiny water droplets collide and form larger drops that fall to the ground. A: rain
Q: Name the type of precipitation: Water vapor freezes into crystals. A: snow	

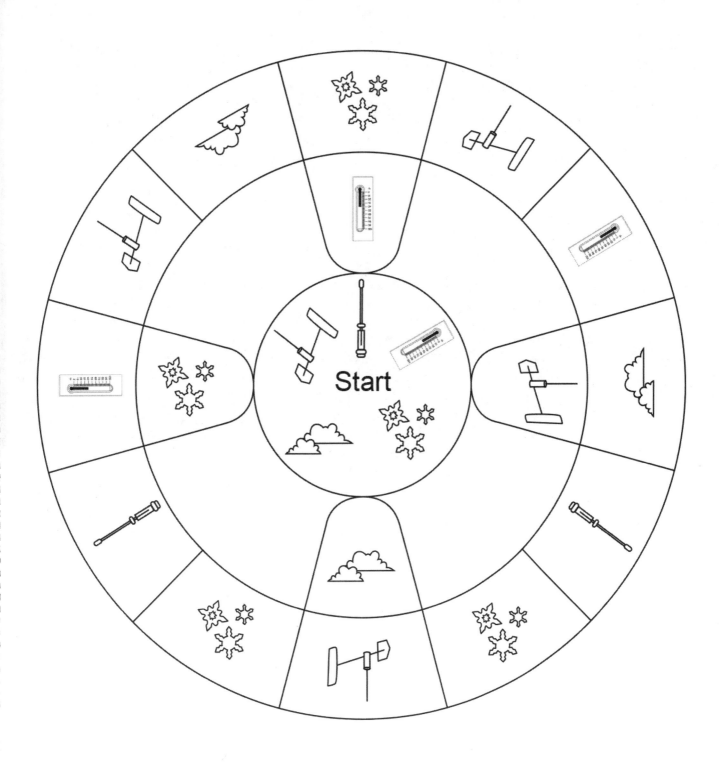

Student Guide
Traveling Light

Light is amazing. Without it, we wouldn't be able to see anything around us. Explore how our world would be different if there were no light. See how light can pass through, be reflected, or be absorbed by an object.

Lesson Objectives

- Explain that when light strikes an object it can reflect, pass through, or be absorbed.
- Classify objects as transparent, opaque, or translucent.

PREPARE

Approximate lesson time is 60 minutes.

Advance Preparation

- Be sure to have a piece of a piece of plastic, preferably a CD case, for the activity.

Materials

For the Student

Tricky Candle

Keywords and Pronunciation

absorb: Take in, but not let out. Like a sponge absorbing water, some things absorb light. A very black object absorbs most of the visible light that hits it.

light: A natural or artificial form of energy that allows us to see. His friend's new bicycle was much easier to see in the light of day than it had been at night.

opaque (oh-PAYK)**:** Not allowing light to pass through, so that objects behind something opaque cannot be seen. He wanted to have an opaque door so that someone outside his room could not easily tell if his light was on.

reflect: Bounce off a surface, as light off a mirror. A perfect mirror reflects all the light that hits it, so that light starting out in one direction can end up going in quite another.

translucent (trans-LOO-snt)**:** Allowing only some light to pass through, and scattering light that does, so that forms behind something translucent cannot be clearly seen. The sunlight passing through the translucent leaves provided enough light for his walk in the woods, even though he couldn't see anything in the sky.

transmit: Pass through. A transparent object transmits all the light that hits it.

transparent: Allowing almost all light to pass through, so that objects behind something transparent can be clearly seen. After his brother cleaned the window, it was so transparent that you could hardly tell it had glass in it.

LEARN

Activity 1: Light Sources *(Online)*

Activity 2: Tricky Candle *(Offline)*

Safety

Be sure to keep the matches out of your student's reach. Do not leave your student unattended with the lighted candle.

ASSESS

Lesson Assessment: Traveling Light *(Online)*

You will complete an online assessment covering the main objectives of this lesson. Sit with your learning coach in case you need help. The assessment will be scored by the computer.

LEARN

Activity 3: Presto Change! *(Online)*

Name _____   Date _____

Traveling Light

Tricky Candle

1. Use two balls of clay to stand up a piece of plastic, such as a CD case, on a flat surface.

2. Place a small candle in another ball of clay 8 inches from the plastic.

3. On the other side, place a clear drinking glass opposite the candle, 8 inches from the plastic.

4. Get help to light the candle, and turn off the lights.

5. Look at the piece of plastic from the candle side and record your observations below.

6. Slowly pour some water into the glass. Look at the piece of plastic again from the candle side. Record your observations below.

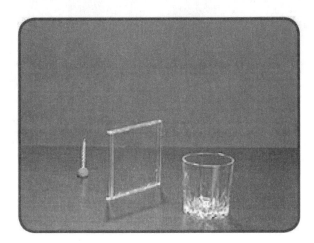

What did you see when you looked at the plastic from the side with the lighted candle?

_____

_____

_____

What happened when you poured water into the glass?

_____

_____

_____

What do you think caused this to happen? Was light being reflected, transmitted, or absorbed by the piece of plastic?

_____

_____

_____

Student Guide
Colors of Light

Is an apple really red, and is the sky really blue? The light shining from a white light bulb may look like one color, but it really holds all the colors of the rainbow. Explore how light can be separated into many colors and mixed together to become white.

Lesson Objectives

- Define refraction as the bending of light as it travels from one type of matter to another.
- State that white light contains all the colors of the rainbow.
- Explain that objects reflect the color of light that we see and absorb the rest.
- State the three primary colors of light: red, green, blue.

PREPARE

Approximate lesson time is 60 minutes.

Advance Preparation

- In this science activity, you will need three flashlights. Your student will also need to cover the flashlights with something to make red, green, and blue light. You can use clear, colored report covers, or colored plastic wrap. The colored plastic wrap produces the best results in this experiment.

Materials

For the Student

Splitting Light
Combining Colors of Light

Keywords and Pronunciation

opaque (oh-PAYK): Not allowing light to pass through, so that objects behind something opaque cannot be seen. He wanted to have an opaque door so that someone outside his room could not easily tell if his light was on.

translucent (trans-LOO-snt): Allowing only some light to pass through, and scattering light that does, so that forms behind something translucent cannot be clearly seen. The sunlight passing through the translucent leaves provided enough light for his walk in the woods, even though he couldn't see anything in the sky.

LEARN

Activity 1: The Colors of Light (Online)

Activity 2: Rainbow Colors (Offline)

Activity 3: Color Combinations (Offline)

ASSESS

Lesson Assessment: Colors of Light (*Online*)

You will complete an online assessment covering the main objectives of the lesson.

LEARN

Activity 4: Optional: Color Wheel (*Offline*)

See if you can trick your brain with this fun experiment.

Activity Steps

1. Cut a circle, 12 centimeters in diameter, out of a piece of white poster board.

2. Draw a light pencil line through the center of the color wheel. Mark the center. Use a pencil to make a hole 1/2 cm. from the center along the line. Then make another hole along the line, the same distance from the center, on the opposite side from the first.

3. Draw seven lines from the center of the circle with a pencil and ruler to make seven triangles, about equal to one another.

4. Color each triangle a different color of the rainbow (red, orange, yellow, green, blue, deep blue, and violet).

5. Push the ends of a piece of string 1 meter long through the two holes. Tie the ends in a knot.

6. Hold the two loops of string with your pointer fingers. Flip the circle around several times to twist up the string.

7. Watch the color side of the wheel as you pull your hands apart to make the color wheel spin around. What happens?

Conclusion

When the color wheel spins very quickly, your eyes actually see all the different colors, but they get mixed up in your brain. When this happens, your brain sees a mixture of all seven colors, which is white.

Name _____ Date _____

Colors of Light
Splitting Light

Did you know that you have the power to split light? Try this activity to test it out.

1. Cut a small, rectangular slit in a 3 x 3 piece of black construction paper, then tape the paper over the end of the flashlight. Be careful not to cover the slit with the tape.

2. Fill a small bowl halfway with water. Lean the mirror at an angle against the side of the bowl so that half of it is underwater and half is above the water's surface. A small piece of modeling clay can be used to hold its bottom in place.

3. With one hand, point the flashlight so that the light beam shines on the mirror under the water.

4. With the other hand, hold up a piece of white paper so that the reflected light shines on the paper.

What did you see projected onto the paper when you shone the white light onto the mirror under the water?

_____

_____

_____

Refraction is light bending as it travels from one type of matter to another. Where did the light from the flashlight refract in this activity?

_____

_____

Name _____   Date _____

Colors of Light
Combining Colors of Light

Follow the instructions.

1. Place six layers of blue plastic wrap over the lighted end of one of the flashlights. Put six layers of red on the second flashlight, and six layers of green on the third.

2. Place a piece of white paper on a fl at surface. With a pencil, make a small dot in the center of the page.

3. Turn out the lights and, with a partner, shine one color at a time on the white piece of paper so that you can see all three colors.

4. Now move the colored circles of light until all three are pointing at the dot you drew on the paper. In the spaces below, record what happens.

   What are the three primary colors of light?

   _____

   _____

   What happened when you shone all three colors on the dot at the same time?

   _____

   _____

   Why did this happen?

   _____

   _____

Student Guide

Light Energy

Have you ever noticed that many people wear bright colors in the summer and darker colors in the winter? Explore how the darkness of the color affects how much light energy is absorbed, as well as how light energy can be converted into heat energy.

Lesson Objectives

- Recognize that when light energy is absorbed it is often changed to heat energy.
- Explain that a dark-colored surface absorbs more visible light than a light-colored surface.
- Explain that a light-colored surface reflects more visible light than a dark-colored surface.

PREPARE

Approximate lesson time is 60 minutes.

Advance Preparation

- A lamp will be used in the experiment so leave one on for ten minutes to warm up. **Note:** The lamp must provide sufficient heat for the experiment. If you can, find the type of bulb, of any wattage, that will provide the heat. If you cannot find one bulb that will heat efficiently, try arranging a number of bulbs until the experiment works. Be creative in finding a heat source that does the job. You will also need two empty tin cans.

Materials

For the Student

Heat It Up!

Keywords and Pronunciation

opaque (oh-PAYK)**:** Not allowing light to pass through, so that objects behind something opaque cannot be seen. He wanted to have an opaque door so that someone outside his room could not easily tell if his light was on.

translucent (trans-LOO-snt)**:** Allowing only some light to pass through, and scattering light that does, so that forms behind something translucent cannot be clearly seen. The sunlight passing through the translucent leaves provided enough light for his walk in the woods, even though he couldn't see anything in the sky.

LEARN

Activity 1: Light Energy *(Online)*

Activity 2: Heat It Up! *(Offline)*

ASSESS

Lesson Assessment: Light Energy (*Online*)

You will complete an online assessment covering the main objectives of the lesson.

LEARN

Activity 3: Optional: It's Melting! (*Offline*)

Overview

Test to see if a shiny surface absorbs more or less light and light energy than a dark-colored surface.

Activity Steps

1. Place six ice cubes in each plastic bag. Place them both under a lamp.

2. Make a tent out of the aluminum foil and black construction paper large enough so that the bags of ice are covered but not touched by the tents.

3. After 15 minutes, lift the paper and foil to see which bag of ice cubes has melted the most.

If there is snow outside, place the paper and aluminum foil on a pile of snow. After ten minutes, use a ruler to see which one has sunk farther into the snow as the snow melted.

Name _____ Date _____

Light Energy

Heat It Up!

Think about what you have learned about colors and light energy. If you place two cans of water under a lamp for 10 minutes, one covered with white paper, and one covered with black paper, which one do you think will heat up the fastest? Write your prediction here.

_____

_____

1. Fill two empty metal cans with water that is the same temperature.

2. Place the thermometer into one of the cans of water and record the temperature on the chart below.

3. Cover the can with a piece of black construction paper. Place the can directly under a lamp for ten minutes.

4. After 10 minutes, lift the paper off the can and take the temperature of the water. Record the temperature on the chart. Find how many degrees the temperature increased while under the lamp and record it.

5. Allow the thermometer to come back to room temperature. Repeat steps 2 to 4, this time using a piece of white construction paper. Be sure to put the second can of water in the same spot you put the first can.

Can	Temperature Before Going Under the Lamp	Temperature After Going Under the Lamp	Number of Degrees the Temperature Increased
Can Covered in Black Paper			
Can Covered in White Paper			

Which can of water heated up the most while under the lamp? Why?

_____

_____

Student Guide

Vision

Do you enjoy watching the explosion of colors during a fireworks display or in a field of beautiful flowers? You can thank your eyes for that. The eye is an amazing organ with many different parts working together to help us see. Learn about the different parts of the eye and how each part has its own special job.

Lesson Objectives

- Recognize that the sense of sight relies on light energy.
- Identify the parts of the eye and their functions (pupil, iris, cornea, lens, retina, optic nerve, rods and cones).

PREPARE

Approximate lesson time is 60 minutes.

Advance Preparation

- Websites and books: As usual, you may wish to preview any books or websites listed in this lesson.

Materials

For the Student

> Parts of the Eye
> Topsy Turvy

Keywords and Pronunciation

Braille (brayl)

cones: Special light-sensitive cells that allow us to see colors and fine detail. Cones are not as sensitive to light as rods, so they need bright light to work well.

cornea: The transparent part of the eye that covers the pupil and the iris.

iris: The colored part of the eye surrounding the pupil.

lens: A transparent structure behind the pupil, with curved surfaces, thicker in the middle than at the edges, that bends light entering the eye to help form images on the retina.

pupil: The opening in the eye through which light enters.

retina (REH-tn-uh)**:** The layer at the back of the eye where light-sensitive cells are found.

rods: Special light-sensitive cells, very sensitive even in dim light. Rods help us see in very dim light, but only in black and white. They are not involved in our seeing of colors or fine detail.

sclera (SKLEHR-uh)

LEARN

Activity 1: The Amazing Eye *(Online)*

Activity 2: The Parts of the Eye *(Offline)*

Activity 3: Topsy Turvy T.V. *(Offline)*

ASSESS

Lesson Assessment: Vision *(Online)*

You will complete an online assessment covering the main objectives of the lesson.

LEARN

Activity 4: A Closer Look at the Eye *(Online)*

Safety

As usual, you may wish to preview any books or websites listed in this lesson.

Name _____ Date _____

Vision

Parts of the Eye

There are many parts of the eye, and each helps with vision. Use the Word Bank below to label the parts of the eye.

Word Bank

lens	cornea	optic nerve
iris	sclera	rods
pupil	retina	cones

Name _____ Date _____

Vision

Topsy Turvy!

Instead of making it larger, let's discover how to turn an image upside down using a magnifying glass.

1. Find a room that has a television.

2. Turn the television on and the lights in the room off.

3. Measure 3 meters from the front of the television.

4. Hold the magnifying glass in one hand and the white paper in the other.

5. Hold the magnifying glass so that it is straight up and down, with the handle out to the side. The magnifying glass should be between the paper and the television screen.

6. Move the paper away from and towards the magnifying glass until you see the image of the television screen on the paper.

   What do you notice about the image?

   _____

   _____

   _____

   _____

Student Guide

Light: Unit Review and Assessment

You have seen a number of interesting things in this unit—thanks to light. Prepare to take the unit assessment by putting on a Light Show and reviewing all the things you have learned.

Lesson Objectives

- Demonstrate mastery of the skills taught in this unit.
- Define refraction as the bending of light as it travels from one type of matter to another.
- Explain that when light strikes an object it can reflect, pass through, or be absorbed.
- Recognize that the sense of sight relies on light energy.
- Explain that a light-colored surface reflects more visible light than a dark-colored surface.
- Explain that objects reflect the color of light that we see and absorb the rest.
- Identify the parts of the eye and their functions (pupil, iris, cornea, lens, retina, optic nerve, rods and cones).

PREPARE

Approximate lesson time is 60 minutes.

Advance Preparation

- Invite friends and/or family to the Light Show. Reuse the printouts from previous activities titled Splitting Light, Combining Colors of Light, and Topsy Turvy.

LEARN

Activity 1: Scavenger Hunt! (Online)

Safety

Accompany your student when he goes outside. Never leave him unattended outside.

Activity 2: Light Show (Offline)

It's time to amaze your friends and family with how much you've learned about light.

First, show them how to separate white light into the colors of the rainbow and how colors can be combined to make white light.

Next, share the Topsy Turvy T.V.! activity and explain how light bends (refracts) when it goes through a lens. Share with them how the "topsy turvy" image created by the lens is like what happens when you see images through the lens of your eye. Also share how the brain doesn't "care" whether the image in the eye is right-side up or upside-down, as long as it "knows" how to use the information to give you your view of the world.

ASSESS

Unit Assessment: Light (Online)

You will complete an online Unit Assessment covering the main objectives of the unit.

Student Guide
Earth and Sun

Lesson Objectives

- Describe the difference between the Earth's movements as it rotates on its axis and revolves around the sun.
- Describe the shape of the earth as being very close to a sphere.
- Identify the shape of the Earth's orbit around the sun as being nearly circular.
- State that the Earth completes one revolution, called an orbit, around the sun each year.
- State that the Earth completes one rotation on its axis every 24 hours.

PREPARE

Approximate lesson time is 60 minutes.

Advance Preparation

- Cook one hard-boiled egg.

Materials

For the Student

Night and Day

Keywords and Pronunciation

axis: a straight line through the center of an object around which it rotates; Earth's axis is an imaginary line that goes through the North and South Poles

orbit: The path of an object as it moves around another object. The Earth's orbit around the sun is nearly circular, with the sun in the middle.

revolution (re-vuh-LOO-shuhn)**:** Movement of an object in an orbit around another object. One complete orbit of the Earth around the sun is called a *revolution*.

rotation: Spinning of an object on an axis.

sphere: The shape of a ball, with every point on the surface the same distance from a center point. Earth's shape is a sphere.

LEARN

Activity 1: The Earth is Moving *(Online)*

Activity 2: Shadows and the Earth *(Offline)*

Safety

This lesson involves eating or working with food. Check with your doctor, if necessary, to find out whether your student will have any allergic reaction to the food.

ASSESS

Lesson Assessment: Earth and Sun (*Online*)

You will complete an online assessment covering the main objectives of the lesson.

LEARN

Activity 3: Optional: Spinning (*Offline*)

Why do the two eggs spin differently? Find out in this activity.

Activity Steps

1. Using a pencil, label the hard-boiled egg # 1. Label the raw egg # 2.
2. Lay the two eggs on a flat surface. A large table or floor without carpet would work best.
3. Spin the first egg (labeled #1) on its side. What do you notice?
4. Spin the second egg (labeled #2) on its side. What do you notice?
5. Why do you think there is a difference in how these two eggs spin?

Answers:

1. The first egg spins easily for a while. It will spin on its own for a few seconds.
2. The second egg wobbles as it is spinning. It spins for a short time and stops quickly.
3. The hard-boiled egg is solid all the way through and the raw egg has liquid and solid inside it. The whole hard-boiled egg spins at once. In the raw egg, the liquid does not start to spin when the shell begins to spin. The liquid does begin to move, but more slowly and unevenly than the shell.

Conclusion:

The Earth is like the raw egg. Portions of it are solid and other portions are liquid. The center of the Earth is a liquid, as is the raw egg's center. The Earth wobbles as it spins, much like the raw egg, but not in as noticeable a way.

Tip: Make sure the two eggs are at room temperature before beginning the activity. Differences in temperature could affect the results.

Name _____ Date _____

Earth and Sun

Night and Day

You will use an orange and a lamp to explore why we have night and day.

Activity Steps

1. Place the pencil through the center of the orange. This represents the axis of the Earth. An *axis* is a line, real or imaginary, that goes through the center of an object, that the object spins around.

2. Trace a line around the orange. That will represent the equator.

3. Set one end of the pencil on the table and, putting your finger on the other end, show that the orange can spin on its axis.

4. Place the orange 30 cm from the lamp. Take the lampshade off so that the light shines directly on the orange.

5. Spin the orange on its axis and notice what happens on both sides of the orange as it is turned.

Like the orange, the Earth spins on an axis, too. For Earth, the axis is an imaginary line that connects the North Pole and the South Pole. One turn of the Earth on its axis is called a *rotation*. It takes about 24 hours for the Earth to rotate once.

6. As you rotate the ball on its axis, move it in a circular path around the lamp.

It takes about 365 days for the Earth to orbit the sun once. This movement of the Earth around the sun is called a *revolution*.

Student Guide
The Seasons

Lesson Objectives

- Explain that the Earth's tilt causes the seasons, partly because the sun shines more directly on the part of the Earth where it's summer and less directly where it's winter.
- Explain that the Earth's tilt causes the seasons, partly because the amount of time the sun shines each day is greater in the summer and less in the winter.
- State that the Earth receives sunlight more directly at the equator than at the poles.
- State that the tilt of the Earth's axis causes the seasons.

PREPARE

Approximate lesson time is 60 minutes.

Materials

For the Student

> *Sunshine Makes the Seasons* Guide
> Centimeter Grid Paper
> *Sunshine Makes the Seasons* by Franklyn M. Branley

Keywords and Pronunciation

axis: a straight line through the center of an object around which it rotates; Earth's axis is an imaginary line that goes through the North and South Poles

equator: An imaginary line around a planet halfway between its North and South Poles. The equator divides the planet into a Northern Hemisphere and a Southern Hemisphere.

season: One of four periods of the year having characteristic average temperature, weather conditions, and length of time the sun shines during a day.

LEARN

Activity 1: Sunshine Makes the Seasons *(Online)*

Safety

This lesson involves eating or working with food. Check with your doctor, if necessary, to find out whether your student will have any allergic reaction to the food.

Activity 2: How Sunlight Strikes the Earth *(Offline)*

Instructions

Overview

Review with your student the idea that when light rays hit a surface from straight above, they are more intense and they heat the surface more. When rays hit at a lower angle, they are spread over a larger area, so each place doesn't get heated as much. Your student will need your help for this activity.

Activity Steps

1. With your student, tape the flashlight along the narrow edge of a ruler. The lighted end of the flashlight should be touching the 5 cm mark. You will need to tape both the bottom and top of the flashlight tightly so that it will stay in place during the activity.

2. Lay the piece of graph paper on a flat surface. In the center of the grid, use a pencil to make an X. Turn the flashlight on and line up the bottom edge of the ruler on one of the lines on the paper so that the beam of light falls on the X.

3. As you hold the flashlight steady, have your student trace the outline of the concentrated part of the beam of light on the graph paper.

4. Then, as you keep the ruler lined up touching the paper in the same place, ease the flashlight to the right until it is about 45 degrees from the paper. Have your student trace the outline of the concentrated part of the beam of light again (it will be larger). Note that the flashlight is the same distance from the X.

5. Ask your student to explain how this shows what happens during the seasons.

Conclusion

The experiment demonstrates that a given portion of the Earth receiving the sun's direct rays gets more concentrated, intense light. The area with the more intense light will have warmer weather, and will be better able to use the sun's light as energy to grow crops, generate electricity, and the like.

ASSESS

Lesson Assessment: The Seasons (*Online*)

You will complete an online assessment covering the main objectives of the lesson.

Name _____ Date _____

The Seasons
Sunshine Makes the Seasons Guide

Overview

This book lesson will help your student understand how seasons result from the Earth's position and motion with regard to the sun. Carefully follow the activity steps, with their respective book page numbers, while you read the book with your student. You will ask your student questions related to the book lesson. You will need a flashlight and a table lamp. Place the lamp in the center of the room and remove the shade.

Activity Steps

1. Page 6: Ask your student to tell you the term that describes the motion of the Earth around the sun. (*Answer:* revolution)

2. Page 9: Ask your student to explain why the days are longer in the summer and shorter in the winter. *Do not be concerned if your student does not answer the question correctly. If your student answers correctly, the following activities will reinforce this understanding. If your student answers incorrectly, the following activities will help clarify any misconceptions about what causes the change in day length.* Read through page 17 before performing the activity.

3. Page 17: After reading through page 17, go back to page 12. Help your student follow along with the text and perform the activity through page 17, using an orange as the Earth model. Make sure your student understands that if the Earth's axis were straight up and down, days and nights would be the same length.

4. Read through page 26, before continuing with the activity. Then go back to page 18 and continue with the activity, reading the instructions below when you reach pages 20 and 25. At the end of this activity, your student should understand that the summer, the sun is higher in the sky and shines for a longer time each day. In the winter it shines less directly and for a shorter time. When the sun is shining on a place on the hemisphere that is tilted torward the sun, the sun is high in the sky and its rays hit that place more directly. The sun's energy, therefore, is more intense, and it warms the place more. And since the sun shines for a longer time each day, the land, oceans, and air can absorb more of the sun's energy and warm up.

- Page 20: Your student should see that the pin is in the light only a short time in this orientation. Your student should pay attention to the position of the "sun" in relationship to the position of the pin. Have your student maintain the tilt of the axis and turn the orange so the pin is facing the lamp. This position represents the noon. Then have your student place the eraser of a pencil on the pin, and point the lead of the pencil toward the sun. The pencil will point at a low angle toward the sun. This angle represents the angle of the rays of sun during the winter, and shows that the sun is low in the sky and shines less directly on that part of the Earth, even at noon. When the sun shines at an angle in the winter, less energy hits the surface of the Earth.
- Page 25: Have your student do the same exercise as for page 20, but notice the difference in the angle of the pencil. Now it points almost straight up. This means that the sun is almost directly overhead at noon, high in the sky. Ask your student to explain how this would affect the intensity of the sun's energy that reaches that point on the Earth in summer. The sun is high in the sky, so its rays hit the Earth more directly and with greater intensity, making temperatures higher in the summer.

5. When you have finished reading the book:

- Have your student do the activity on page 30 to reinforce the idea that at the equator, the length of time the sun shines and the length of time spent in darkness are the same year-round—and, second, the length of time the sun shines in a day varies the most at the poles.
- Reinforce the idea that the seasons are reversed in the Northern and Southern Hemispheres. To help you do this, have your student name the summer months at home, then the summer months somewhere in the opposite hemisphere. (e.g., Chile for a Northern Hemisphere resident). Then do the same for the winter months. (*Answer*: Summer in Southern Hemisphere is January–March. Winter is July–September).
- Ask your student to explain the two main reasons that the tilt of the Earth's axis causes changes in seasons. (*Answers*: The tilt of the Earth's axis causes (1) the sun to shine more directly on some parts of the Earth, contributing to the higher temperatures during the local summer, and less directly on other parts of the Earth, contributing to the lower temperatures in the local winter; and (2) differences in the length of time the sun shines during a day. The places where the sun shines longer get energy for a longer time each day.

Name   Date

Centimeter Grid Paper

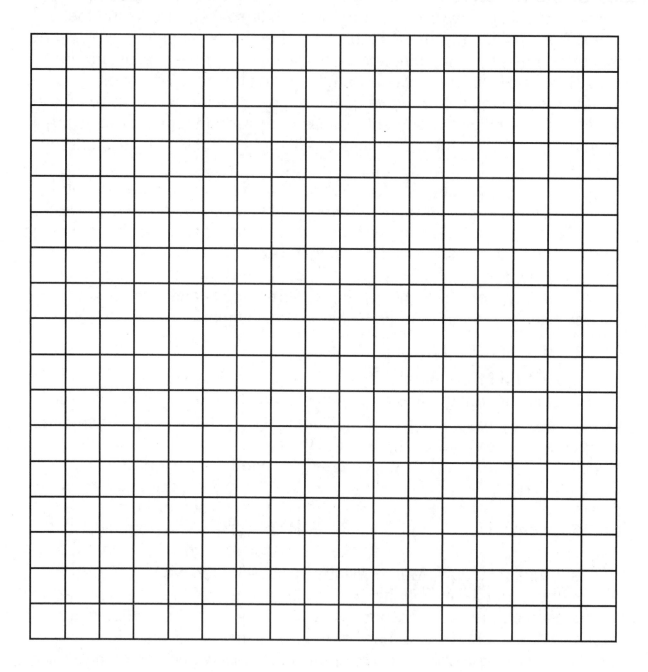

Student Guide
Phases of the Moon

Lesson Objectives

- State that the moon makes one revolution around Earth, and one rotation on its own axis, in approximately one month.
- Demonstrate mastery of the skills taught in this lesson.
- Identify the moon's phases: new, crescent, quarter, gibbous, and full.
- Recognize that the moon's phases are the result of our seeing different amounts of the moon's lighted side from our position on the Earth.
- State that the moon does not produce its own light, but that the moon is visible from Earth because sunlight reflects off its surface.
- State the order of the moon's phases from one new moon to the next (new, crescent, first quarter, gibbous, full, gibbous, third quarter, crescent, new).

PREPARE

Approximate lesson time is 60 minutes.

Materials

For the Student

    The Moon Seems to Change Guide
    Moon Phases Calendar
    The Moon Seems to Change by Franklyn M. Branley

Keywords and Pronunciation

gibbous (JIH-buhs)

lunar cycle: The repeating pattern of changes in the appearance of the moon as it goes through its various phases.

satellite: A body that orbits a planet. The moon is a natural satellite that orbits the Earth.

LEARN

Activity 1: The Moon Seems to Change *(Online)*

Safety

As usual, you may wish to preview any books or websites listed in this lesson.

This lesson involves eating or working with food. Check with your doctor, if necessary, to find out whether your student will have any allergic reaction to the food.

Activity 2: A Month of Phases *(Online)*

ASSESS

Lesson Assessment: Phases of the Moon *(Online)*

You will complete an online assessment covering the main objectives of the lesson.

Name _____   Date _____

Phases of the Moon
The Moon Seems to Change Guide

I. Book Reading

Read *The Moon Seems to Change* by Franklyn Branley with your student. At page 19, stop and review with your student the topics and bulleted items listed below. These points will help your student understand and remember the material presented in this lesson, as well as the material in the previous lessons.

A. Rotation and Revolution

1. Ask your student to state the difference between rotation and revolution. (*Answers*: *Rotation* is the spinning of an object on its own axis. *Revolution* is the motion of one object around another. The Earth revolves around the sun, while the moon revolves around the Earth.)

2. Make sure your student understands that, like the Earth, the moon also rotates (spins) on its axis.

3. Ask your student how long it takes the Earth to rotate one full turn. (*Answer:* about 24 hours) Ask how long it takes the moon to rotate one full turn. (*Answer:* about one month)

4. Make sure your student understands that it also takes the moon about one month to revolve around the Earth. It takes the Earth one year (about 365 days) to revolve around the sun.

5. The fact that it takes the moon the same amount of time to revolve once around the Earth and to rotate once on its axis explains why we always see the same side of the moon. Your student may have trouble understanding this concept at first, but it should become clear as your student completes the activities in the lesson.

Teacher Tip:

One way to help make clear that it involves rotation is to have your student move around something while always facing it. Doing this, your student will be revolving and rotating at the same rate. Have your student come closer and closer to the object until it becomes clear that near the center point one is clearly rotating.

B. The Moon's Light

1. Explain to your student that the moon does not produce its own light. The moon is not a source of light. It is visible from Earth because sunlight reflects off its surface. Ask your student how this is different from the sun. (*Answer:* It is different because the sun produces its own light. Point out that this difference is evident from the much greater brightness of the sun.)

C. The Moon Phases

1. Remind your student that the moon phases occur in a repeating pattern. What we see from here on Earth is a result of how the Earth, moon, and sun are positioned in relation to each other.

2. Ask your student to state the order of the moon phases from one new moon to the next. (*Answer:* New moon, crescent, first quarter, gibbous, full, gibbous, third quarter, crescent, and new moon)

3. Point out to your student that often when there is a crescent moon, the rest of the moon can be dimly seen because light reflects off the Earth and back to the moon. If you have a clear night with a crescent moon, observe this phenomenon.

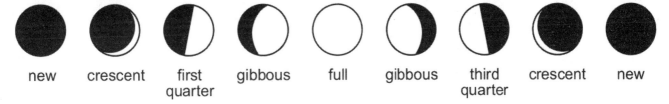

new   crescent   first quarter   gibbous   full   gibbous   third quarter   crescent   new

D. The Gibbous Moon

1. Your student will be learning one moon phase that is not discussed in this book—the gibbous (JIH-buhs) phase. This lesson introduces the gibbous phase and addresses it in later activities. Describe this phase to your student. (Note that it is the phase shown in the 5th and 6th pictures of the waxing moon on page 8, and in the 2nd and 3rd of the waning moon.)

2. The moon in the gibbous phase is not completely full, but looks larger than a quarter moon. A gibbous moon occurs between the first quarter and the full moon, and again between the full moon and the third quarter. Look at the circled moons in the illustration. That's the gibbous moon in both stages.

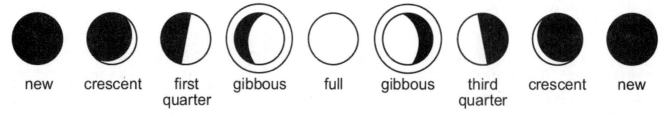

new   crescent   first   gibbous   full   gibbous   third   crescent   new
                   quarter   quarter

Now that you've reviewed the material from the book, begin reading again at page 20.

II. Book Activity

A. Begin

1. Begin the activity described in your book on pages 20-29. You will be using an orange to represent the moon. Be sure to clarify with your student that this is different from the way you used the orange last lesson when it represented the Earth.

B. Tips for Activity:

1. This activity works best in a dark room. Use a lamp with the shade removed. If the windows do not have heavy shades, cover them with black-plastic garbage bags.

2. Make sure your student holds the model of the moon up high so your student's own shadow does not cover it during the full-moon phase. The Earth's shadow on the moon (the shadow of your student's head on the model moon) would demonstrate an eclipse, which will be discussed in the next lesson.

Your student may find it difficult to visualize the moon phases. You may wish to repeat this activity the next day or at the beginning of the next Science lesson. Or, have your student draw in the moon phases in the Science Notebook as they are observed.

Phases of the Moon
Moon Phase Calendar

Sunday	Monday	Tuesday	Wednesday	Thursday	Friday	Saturday
Date: ___	Date: ___	Date: ___	Date: ___	Date: ___	Date: ___	Date: ___
What I see:	What I see:	What I see:	What I see:	What I see:	What I see:	What I see:
Date: ___	Date: ___	Date: ___	Date: ___	Date: ___	Date: ___	Date: ___
What I see:	What I see:	What I see:	What I see:	What I see:	What I see:	What I see:

Sunday	Monday	Tuesday	Wednesday	Thursday	Friday	Saturday
Date: _____ What I see:	Date: _____ What I see:	Date: _____ What I see:	Date: _____ What I see:	Date: _____ What I see:	Date: _____ What I see:	Date: _____ What I see:
Date: _____ What I see:	Date: _____ What I see:	Date: _____ What I see:	Date: _____ What I see:	Date: _____ What I see:	Date: _____ What I see:	Date: _____ What I see:

Student Guide
Eclipses

Lesson Objectives

- Define *eclipse* as the darkening of a planet, moon, or other object in space by the shadow of another object in space.
- Describe the positions of the Earth, moon, and sun during a lunar eclipse (the Earth, between the sun and the moon, blocks the sunlight and casts a shadow on the moon).
- Describe the positions of the Earth, moon, and sun during a solar eclipse (the moon, between the sun and the Earth, blocks the sunlight and casts a shadow on the Earth).

PREPARE

Approximate lesson time is 60 minutes.

Keywords and Pronunciation

eclipse: The darkening of a planet, moon, or other object in space by the shadow of another object in space.

lunar eclipse: The darkening of part or all of the moon by the shadow of the Earth, when the Earth is between the sun and the moon. Amy saw a lunar eclipse in the sky and knew it resulted from the Earth sitting between the sun and the moon.

opaque (oh-PAYK)**:** Not allowing light to pass through, so that objects behind something opaque cannot be seen. He wanted to have an opaque door so that someone outside his room could not easily tell if his light was on.

solar eclipse: The darkening of a place on the Earth by the moon's shadow, when the moon is between the sun and the Earth. Josh pointed to the solar eclipse and explained to his friends that the eclipse was caused when the moon is between the Earth and the sun.

LEARN

Activity 1: Lunar and Solar Eclipses *(Online)*

Activity 2: How Does an Eclipse Happen? *(Offline)*

Safety

This lesson involves eating or working with food. Before beginning, check with your doctor, if necessary, to find out whether your student will have any allergic reactions to the food.

ASSESS

Lesson Assessment: Eclipses *(Online)*

You will complete an offline assessment covering the main objectives of this lesson. Sit with your learning coach in case you need help. The assessment will be scored by the computer

LEARN

Activity 3: Optional: Upcoming Eclipses *(Online)*

Safety

As usual, you may wish to preview the websites listed in this lesson.

Never look directly into the sun.

Student Guide
Lunar Landscape
Lesson Objectives

- Describe how a crater is formed on the moon.
- Identify and describe some characteristics of the moon's surface: craters, maria (lowland plains), rilles (valleys), highlands, and soil.
- State that the moon's surface has no air, wind, liquid water, or life.

PREPARE

Approximate lesson time is 60 minutes.

Advance Preparation

- If you don't already have it, you will need *The Moon Book* by Gail Gibbons. (New York: Holiday House, 1997) for the optional activity in this lesson.

Materials

For the Student

Create Some Craters!

Keywords and Pronunciation

craters: Depressions on the surface caused by impacts of objects hitting the surface, usually with raised rims.

Galileo Galilei (gal-uh-LEE-oh gal-uh-LAY-ee)

maria (MAHR-ee-uh)**:** Low areas covered with rocky soil on the surface of the moon. Singular: mare (MAH-ray).

rilles (rilz)**:** Long, narrow cracks or valleys on the surface of the moon.

LEARN

Activity 1: The Surface of the Moon *(Online)*

Activity 2: Create Some Craters! *(Offline)*

Safety

Wear safety goggles while performing this activity.

This lesson involves eating or working with food. Check with your doctor, if necessary, to find out whether your student will have any allergic reaction to the food.

ASSESS

Lesson Assessment: Lunar Landscape *(Online)*

You will complete an online assessment covering the main objectives of the lesson.

LEARN

Activity 3: Optional: The Mysterious Moon *(Online)*

Name _____   Date _____

Lunar Landscape
Create Some Craters!

Overview

How does the size of an asteroid or meteoroid affect the size of the crater it leaves when it hits the surface of the moon? In this activity, you will be dropping different-sized asteroids and meteoroids (different-sized round objects) onto the surface of the moon (a pan full of flour). Write down your prediction in the space below for which round object you think will make the biggest crater.

I predict the _____ will make the biggest crater.

Activity Steps

1. Place several sheets of newspaper on the floor to spread out over at least a 2m x 2m space. Put the baking pan in the center of the newspapers.

2. Pour about 2100mL (9 cups) of flour into the pan. Use the edge of your ruler to make the surface of the flour as smooth as possible. Be sure not to press down on the flour, as it should be loose and powdery.

3. Sprinkle cocoa into the pan to cover the surface of the flour. The cocoa will help you see the craters you make more clearly.

4. Stand the ruler next to the pan. Drop the largest ball from a height of 30 cm into the pan. Leave it there as you do the same thing with the other two balls.

5. Carefully remove the balls from the pan without touching the area around them.

6. Use your ruler to measure the diameter (how far across) of the crater made by each of the balls and record it on the chart below.

7. Measure how deep each crater is and record it on the table.

Name of round object	Diameter of the crater	Depth of the crater

Which of the "asteroids" made the crater with the largest diameter? Was your prediction correct?

_____

_____

Which one made the deepest crater?

_____

_____

Did the biggest "asteroid" make the deepest crater? Explain why or why not (hint: think about the mass of each of the objects).

_____

_____

How were the craters you made in the flour like the craters that are made by asteroids and meteoroids on the surface of the moon?

_____

_____

Extension

Have your student choose one of the balls and repeat the activity again, this time dropping the ball each time from a different height. Then discuss the changes that take place when dropping the ball from different heights.

Student Guide

Optional: Origin of the Moon

Lesson Objectives

- Identify the moon as a natural satellite of Earth, held in orbit by the force of gravity.
- Recognize how the the *large-impact* hypothesis explains the formation of the moon.

PREPARE

Approximate lesson time is 60 minutes.

Materials

For the Student

Around and Around

Keywords and Pronunciation

satellite: An object orbiting around a larger one. The moon is a natural satellite that orbits the Earth.

LEARN

Activity 1: Optional: Lesson Instructions (*Online*)

This lesson is OPTIONAL. It is provided for students who seek enrichment or extra practice. You may skip this lesson.

If you choose to skip this lesson, then go to the Plan or Lesson Lists page and mark this lesson "Skipped" in order to proceed to the next lesson in the course.

Activity 2: Optional: Origin of the Moon (*Online*)

Activity 3: Optional: Around and Around (*Offline*)

Safety

Complete this activity in a large, open area. Caution your student to be careful when swinging the ball over her head.

Name _____   Date _____

Origin of the Moon
Around and Around

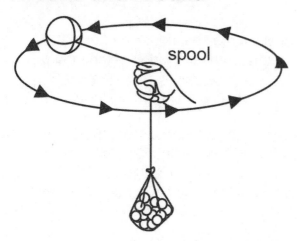

spool

1. Tie one end of a 1-meter long piece of string to a ball and tape the string down to secure it. Thread the other end through the center of a spool of thread.

2. Fill a resealable sandwich bag with enough marbles so that the bag is heavier than the ball.

3. Tie the other end of the string to the bag of marbles.

4. Move to a big, open space. Hold the spool of thread in one hand and the bag of marbles in the other.

5. Carefully begin to move the spool in a circular motion above your head to start the ball moving.

6. Keep the spool moving as you release the bag of marbles. Observe what happens to the bag and ball as the spool spins.

What happened to the ball as you started to move the spool?

_____

_____

_____

What is the name of the force that helps keep the moon in orbit around the Earth?

_____

_____

_____

_____

Student Guide

Sun, Earth, and Moon: Unit Review and Assessment

Lesson Objectives

- Demonstrate mastery of the skills taught in this unit.
- Explain that the Earth's tilt causes the seasons, partly because the sun shines more directly on the part of the Earth where it's summer and less directly where it's winter.
- State that the moon makes one revolution around Earth, and one rotation on its own axis, in approximately one month.
- Describe the positions of the Earth, moon, and sun during a lunar eclipse (the Earth, between the sun and the moon, blocks the sunlight and casts a shadow on the moon).
- Describe the positions of the Earth, moon, and sun during a solar eclipse (the moon, between the sun and the Earth, blocks the sunlight and casts a shadow on the Earth).
- Identify and describe some characteristics of the moon's surface: craters, maria (lowland plains), rilles (valleys), highlands, and soil.
- State that the Earth completes one revolution, called an orbit, around the sun each year.
- State that the Earth completes one rotation on its axis every 24 hours.
- State that the moon does not produce its own light, but that the moon is visible from Earth because sunlight reflects off its surface.
- State that the moon's surface has no air, wind, liquid water, or life.
- State the order of the moon's phases from one new moon to the next (new, crescent, first quarter, gibbous, full, gibbous, third quarter, crescent, new).

PREPARE

Approximate lesson time is 60 minutes.

Materials

For the Student

Exploring the Sun, Earth, and Moon Guide

LEARN

Activity 1: Explore the Sun, Earth, and Moon *(Online)*

ASSESS

Unit Assessment: Changes in the States of Matter *(Online)*

You will complete an online Unit Assessment covering the main objectives of the unit.

Name _____   Date _____

Sun, Earth and Moon: Unit Review and Assessment
Exploring the Sun, Earth, and Moon Guide

Overview

As an activity and for review, your student will be asked to take notes while reading through the Explore section. Your student can then use these notes to make a presentation about the sun, Earth, and moon to friends and family.

The following information will help you guide your student through the review which lists the key points that your student may want to address.

Screen 3:

Remind your student that the material covered in the lesson titled Earth and Sun can be used to help remember important points. Listed below are the main points. You may need to help with these while your student responds in the notebook.

- The Earth spins around, or *rotates*, on its axis. It takes about 24 hours for the Earth to rotate once. The half of the Earth that is facing the sun has daylight. The opposite side is in darkness. When it is nighttime, the Earth blocks the light from the sun. We are then in the Earth's shadow.
- While the Earth rotates it is also revolving around the sun. It takes one year (about 365 days) for the Earth to revolve completely around the sun.

Screen 4:

Remind your student to use the Explore in the lesson titled The Seasons, as well as the book *Sunshine Makes the Seasons*, to help write explanations. Listed below are the main points. You may need to help your student with responses in the notebook.

- The hemisphere that is tilted towards the sun receives the sun's rays more directly, which makes the energy more intense. This makes the seasonal temperature higher. This is one reason this hemisphere experiences summer. The hemisphere that is tilted away from the sun receives the sun's rays less directly, at a lower angle to the surface. This makes the energy spread out over a larger area, and thus makes it less intense in any one spot. Therefore the seasonal temperatures are lower. This is one reason this hemisphere experiences winter.
- The tilt also has an effect on how long portions of the Earth are exposed to sunlight during the day. The hemisphere that is tilted towards the sun,

experiencing summer, is exposed to sunlight for a longer time each day, and is darker for a shorter time. This contributes to the warmer weather in summer. The hemisphere that is tilted away from the sun, experiencing winter, is exposed to sunlight for a shorter time each day, and is darker for a longer time. This contributes to the cooler weather in winter.

Screen 5

Remind your student to use the Explore in the lesson titled Phases of the Moon to help write explanations. Below are the main points. You may need to help your student with responses in the notebook.

- It takes the moon about one month to revolve around the Earth. It takes the moon the same time to rotate fully on its axis. We always see the same side of the moon from Earth because the moon rotates and revolves at the same rate.
- The moon and the Earth are similar in that each rotates on its axis and revolves around another object. The moon revolves around the Earth and the Earth revolves around the sun.
- The moon does not produce its own light. The moon is visible from Earth because sunlight reflects (bounces) off its surface.

Screen 6

Remind your student, if necessary, to use the lesson titled Moon Phases and Eclipses, as well as the book *The Moon Seems to Change*, to help write explanations. Below are the main points. You may need to help your student with responses in the notebook.

- The order of the moon's phases from one new moon to the next is: new moon, crescent, first quarter, gibbous, full moon, gibbous, third quarter, crescent, new moon.
- Your student should be able to identify the moon's phases from pictures: new, crescent, quarter, gibbous, and full.
- A lunar eclipse occurs when the Earth is between the sun and the moon, so the Earth blocks sunlight and casts its shadow on the moon.
- A solar eclipse occurs when the moon is between the sun and the Earth, so the moon blocks sunlight and casts its shadow on the Earth.

Screen 7

Remind your student to use the Explore in the lesson titled Lunar Landscape to help write explanations. Check the answers to the questions onscreen are provided. You may need to help your student with responses in the notebook.